If these are
laugh lines,
I'm having
way too much fun

If these are
laugh lines,
I'm having
way too much fun

Rose Madeline Mula

PELICAN PUBLISHING COMPANY
GRETNA 2006

*The word "Pelican" and the depiction of a pelican are trademarks
of Pelican Publishing Company, Inc., and are registered in the
U.S. Patent and Trademark Office.*

Library of Congress Cataloging-in-Publication Data

Mula, Rose Madeline.
    If these are laugh lines, I'm having way too much fun / Rose
Madeline Mula.
        p. cm.
    ISBN-13: 978-1-58980-377-0 (pbk. : alk. paper)
    1. Aging—Humor. 2. American wit and humor. I. Title.
    PN6231.A43M86 2006
    305.26'0207—dc22

                                        2006004229

Printed in the United States of America

Published by Pelican Publishing Company, Inc.
1000 Burmaster Street, Gretna, Louisiana 70053

For Madeline, Alexandra, and Jonathan, the joys of my life

Contents

Preface and Acknowledgments

This book is for everyone who, like me, has reached the age where mirrors have become the enemy. I avoid mine scrupulously. I don't want to see the strange old lady who's lurking there. Okay, I know that's crazy. Logically, I realize that I'm the crone in that cursed piece of glass, but how can that be? Wasn't it just yesterday that I was a teenager?

I tell myself that the grooves in my face aren't wrinkles, they're laugh lines. Well, if that's true, I'm having way too much fun. On second thought, there's no such thing as *too much* fun. Therefore, since I can't stop the aging process and all of life's other vexing situations, I'm trying to laugh at them. I hope this book will help you do the same.

My sincere thanks to my relatives and friends for their encouragement and for providing much of the grist for my mill. Even though I have avoided identifying most of them by name in these essays, I'm sure they will recognize themselves. Hopefully, they will continue to speak to me (and not to their attorneys).

Above all, my deepest appreciation for the invaluable support and enthusiasm of the dedicated staff at Pelican Publishing Company with whom I have worked, including Joseph Billingsley, Amy Kirk, Nina Kooij, Frank McGuire, Karen Robicheaux, and Mel Tarman. This book would not have been possible without their incomparable professionalism, proficiency, and incredible good humor.

If these are **laugh lines,** I'm having way too much fun

Who's That Old Fogey Who Claims to Be Me?

I have a problem that's driving me crazy. A while back, a strange old woman moved into my house—uninvited—and took up residence in all my mirrors. As if that wasn't bad enough, she has now completely taken over my life, my possessions, my very identity.

She has added a roll of flab around my middle, she cancelled my subscription to *Cosmo* and enrolled me in AARP, and she even dumped my cute boyfriend and replaced him with a white-haired guy I don't even recognize. All of this has made my own hair turn gray.

She also actually traded in my red two-door sports car for a sedate black sedan. Guess why? She says it's much more appropriate, since I'll be going to lots of funerals from now on. When I asked her what makes her think so, she said I have to get real and face the fact that most of my pals will soon be heading for that great Senior Center in the Sky—and if I don't beat them to it, I can't very well see them off in a red car.

She used the same reasoning to defend removing all traces of them from my address book and inserting instead only strangers, all of whom have *M.D.* after their names.

She constantly complains about "kids today" and all the sex, violence, and rap music on TV, the movies, and the radio. In fact, she keeps my radios at home and in the car tuned to a station that plays unbelievably corny songs called "Golden Oldies."

She really embarrasses me when I go to the movies, the theater, or a restaurant by loudly demanding a senior discount. I'd gladly slip her a few bucks myself if she would just shut up.

She even had the nerve to toss out all my gorgeous high-heeled shoes. She says she can't walk on them because of her corns and bunions.

My bikinis have also disappeared, as have all my shorts, miniskirts, and tank tops. Is it my fault that she let her stomach, thighs, and upper arms get so flabby she has to keep them covered?

My designer jeans are gone, too. She expects me to wear ugly, elastic-waist stretch pants instead—and with baggy, shapeless tops that even women who are nine months pregnant would scoff at.

She couldn't understand why I refused to wear Reeboks last New Year's Eve. She said what difference did it make what I wore since I'd just be sitting at home in front of the TV watching that silly ball drop in Times Square. And whose fault is that? If she wasn't cramping my style, I could have been hitting the high spots with a hip, young crowd; but they didn't invite me because they know she would have insisted on tagging along.

She has put a serious crimp in my social life—and not just on New Year's Eve. No more bar hopping, dances, and all-night parties, ever. Her idea of a good time is to sit around and play Scrabble with her contemporaries . . . and I'm not even allowed to complain when one of them wins all the time.

She even turns off my TV at ten o'clock every night and insists I go right to bed. I wouldn't mind, but then she keeps me awake and gets me up to go to the bathroom every couple of hours.

She does exercise—I'll give her that—but she tore up my

membership to the trendy gym I used to patronize, and she gave my hunky personal trainer the boot. Instead, she enrolled me in a strength-training class at the Senior Center. The Senior Center! That's for old people! I certainly don't belong there. In fact, it upsets me so much that I sometimes can't keep up with the rest of the class. I'm certainly more fit than they are, but I use up all my energy seething in anger over the way that old fogey has disrupted my existence.

She's replaced all the good food in my kitchen with reduced-fat, low-cholesterol, no-taste fiber. She's driving me to drink, but all she'll allow me is an occasional glass of wine. Goodbye margaritas, piña coladas, and mudslides.

Even though she has somehow managed to crease my face like an accordion, in my head I'm still seventeen, and I look like Catherine Zeta-Jones—only younger. But when I tell her that, she laughs hysterically and tells me I'm delusional.

Unfortunately, it's clear that she has no intention of leaving. I can't kick her out. Where would she go? I'm not heartless, after all; so I guess I have no choice but to learn to live with her.

They say "if you can't beat 'em, join 'em," but that's simply not an option for me. However, maybe I can get *her* to join *me*— or at least meet me halfway. Compromise could be the solution.

I could start by not fighting her about the shoes if she'll let me watch TV until eleven o'clock a couple of nights a week. (To tell you the truth—though I won't go so far as admitting it to her—it's a relief to get out of those blasted high heels.)

Be It Ever So Humble

Yesterday I drove by my old homestead or, I should say, one of my old homesteads—specifically, the one my family and I moved into when I was eleven and out of when I was sixteen.

Actually, *old homestead* is not accurate, since that term conjures up images of a gracious manor with stately columns, a wide veranda, and acres of green lawn.

Not even close. This particular dwelling was a small, cramped apartment over a bakery shop that my mother and aunt operated during World War II, while my uncle was fighting the Axis Menace in Salerno and Anzio and my dad, who was too old for the draft, was working on an assembly line in a local defense plant.

Bakery is as much of a misnomer as *homestead,* since none of the products offered for sale was baked on the premises. They were supplied, as part of the sales deal, by the former owner, who had opened a new bakeshop across town. The man had no imagination whatsoever. His idea of a holiday confection was his everyday, plebeian loaf cake "decorated" with a single word in block print: THANKSGIVING, HALLOWEEN, EASTER— whatever special day the calendar proclaimed. Maybe he wasn't artistic and didn't know how to make little icing rosettes or turkeys, pumpkins, or bunnies; but would it have killed him to at least slap the word HAPPY in front of the holiday ID?

His other products were equally unappealing. The pies all had concave centers, the cakes were lopsided, the sugar cookies soggy, and the brownies crisp and dry. I can remember my mother and aunt constantly rearranging these disasters in the display window, desperately seeking configurations that would hide their defects. An impossible dream. My mom would then stand by the window all day, watching the goods go stale, her brow furrowed, her mouth grim. I'm still not sure which discouraged customers more—the unpalatable pastries or my mother's scowl. She got to practice it a lot, since the store was open from 8:00 A.M. to 10:00 P.M., six days a week.

No vacations. No sick leave. No pension plan. No holiday bonuses. The only "perk" was all the unappealing stale pastry we could eat.

Certainly the upstairs apartment couldn't qualify as a benefit. It consisted of a kitchen, one bathroom, and three other rooms, all of which had to serve as bedrooms. I was taking piano lessons; and since we had no living room, I had to share my small bedroom with a large upright. It loomed over my tiny bed, and I was half-convinced it would crush me in my sleep if I didn't practice my requisite hour per day.

Finally, after five years of red ink instead of sweet profits, my family decided to cut their losses and sell the store, along with the less-than-palatial living quarters above it. O happy day!

A variety of small businesses have occupied those premises since then—a produce stand, a convenience store, a photocopy center, and most recently a fishing-tackle shop.

When I drove by yesterday, I saw a large sign outside what used to be my bedroom window. It read LIVE BAIT.

Talk about your humble beginnings.

Clothes Encounters

Recently I was walking by the local high school at the closing bell. As I watched swarms of kids spilling out the doors, I wondered if someone had laced my lunch yogurt with LSD. Or maybe I had somehow wandered onto the set of a movie whose costume designer had gone berserk.

Something was definitely wrong with this picture. Earrings, nose rings, eyebrow rings, bizarre hair-dos, purple nail polish . . . on the boys. Even weirder, one of them was actually wearing a bathrobe and slippers. I swear. The others sported second-skin-tight Spandex bicycle shorts or kaleidoscopic, ridiculously baggy pants obviously stolen from Barnum & Bailey. Topping these were huge sweatshirts emblazoned with obscene slogans and very graphic graphics.

As for the girls, most of them looked as if they had just sashayed off the runway of the old burlesque house. I could not believe they had been allowed into school in those snug, crotch-high skirts, necklines that dipped to their navels, and combat boots. Where were the modest plaid skirts, bow-tied blouses, and shiny loafers my girlfriends and I wore to high school? Probably in the Smithsonian along with the boys' neatly pressed corduroy trousers, white shirts, and argyle socks.

When I got home I pulled out the old family photo albums to see if maybe my memory had finally deserted me completely.

Could our clothes really have been so different from those of today's kids? Ah, yes. There we were, all gussied up, in those black and white Brownie photo prints with the curlicue edges. Those were the post-depression years, so none of us was well heeled; but we certainly were well dressed. And well coiffed. The grammar-school me smiled shyly at the camera, my long banana curls clipped in place with a huge taffeta bow. I was wearing my favorite puffed-sleeved Shirley Temple frock, ankle socks, and gleaming patent-leather Mary Janes. My girlfriends looked equally ladylike. And the boys—all natty and neat in their knickers, knee socks, and newly shorn heads. No pony-tails, dreadlocks, or Mohawks. Fortunately. If a boy had walked into class with any of the above, the teacher would have flat-lined before she had a chance to send him to the principal's office.

I turned a few pages. We were now older but no less fashion-able. Even our "play" clothes looked as though we could never have actually played in them. So stylish. So clean. So pressed!

A few more pages, and we were teenagers, with glamorous hair-dos, fake-fur-trimmed coats, and high heels (the girls, not the boys). As for them—not a bathrobe in the bunch. But maybe we just always dressed up for the camera. No. Thinking back, I recall that we weren't adorned for special picture-taking occasions; the photos simply chronicled our everyday attire. I have snapshots of me in my going-to-college wardrobe, for example— beautiful wool suits, dresses and jumpers, nylons and pumps. Jeans? Are you kidding? Even tailored slacks would have gotten me expelled.

At that point, the albums ran out. No more snapshots. We had graduated to 35-millimeter slides. I pulled some out and set up the screen and projector. Our images were now in large, living color, but our wardrobes hadn't changed.

Look! There I was with my girlfriends on Fifth Avenue, our

first trip to New York . . . and there, on the Champs Elysées, our first trip to Europe . . . in dresses, hats, white gloves, and— heaven help us—those blasted high heels, in which we walked for miles in agonizing pain. You know what I wished for when I threw my coin in the Trevi Fountain? I wished I could throw my shoes in the Trevi Fountain. If only I had. It would have saved me years of podiatrists' bills.

I bet that boy who goes to school in his slippers doesn't have tormented toes like mine. Maybe he's got the right idea after all.

Tomorrow I'm wearing Reeboks to church. So what if it's my grandniece's wedding. If the bridesmaids can do it, so can I.

Quiet, Please!

Will someone please turn down the volume on the planet? Why is it so *loud?* Where's the remote? I can't stand this din a minute longer.

Does the word "tinnitus" ring a bell? It's a wonder any of us has any hearing left at all. How long will it be before we all become deaf as the Sphinx because of the noise pollution that permeates our environment?

Okay, so some of it serves a purpose. In the case of the cacophony of police and ambulance sirens and smoke alarms, for example, the benefits outweigh the potential damage to our eardrums. But other noise sources such as blaring stereos and ultra-sensitive car alarms that shriek even when no burglary is in progress (and which everyone ignores) have no redeeming value.

When did it all happen? It wasn't like this in 1697. No, I don't remember personally, but William Congreve wrote back then that "music hath charms to soothe the savage breast." Today, on the other hand, much of what passes for music sounds as if it emanates from savage beasts. Instead of enchanting, harmonious melodies, we hear raucous roars, screeching screams, and dissonant discord that assault us from our neighbors' CD players, car radios on the highway, boom boxes on the streets and beaches, and even loudspeaker systems in shopping malls, restaurants, and bars. It's impossible to carry on a conversation anywhere. And when we try, we only add to the din as we all bellow to make ourselves heard. The more ear-splitting the "music," the louder we yell.

There is no escape. Whatever you do, don't make the mistake of slipping into a movie theater for some respite from the roar of the crowd. The features are noisy enough, but much worse are the clamorous, surround-sound previews. Why must they turn the decibels up to maximum volume when showing a blurry kaleidoscope of the most violent scenes from future attractions? It's downright painful. I've asked ushers and managers roving the lobby about this, and the answer is always the same: "People like it." Really? Then how come I see so many in the audience blocking their ears and wincing? Actually, it's a turnoff. If I hate the sample, I certainly won't be tempted to see the entire film. These days when I decide to go to a movie, it's usually in spite of—not because of—the preview.

If the hullabaloo continues to escalate, the next generation of toddlers will be wearing hearing aids to preschool, where they will learn sign language. Before long, all noise will end. Talking will become obsolete since we won't be able to hear what anyone says, music will just be something people will read about in history books, and silent movies will make a big comeback. The good news is that there will be no need to buy costly quadra-phonic sound systems for every room in the house, and cars will be less expensive because they won't have sophisticated audio systems and horns.

I'm almost looking forward to it.

Piano Blues

If a woman of seventy goes back to college to get her degree and makes the cheerleading squad as well, the world applauds her ambition and vitality. If a grandmother of five takes up skydiving, everyone envies her youthful verve. However, if you decide to study piano at an age when your contemporaries are honing their rocking-chair techniques, people think you're really off yours—your rocker, that is.

"The piano? At your age?" my friends scoffed when I confided my plan. "With those arthritic fingers? And your shriveling brain?" The taunts would have discouraged me had I not impulsively invested a chunk of my retirement fund in a lovely spinet to complement my living-room decor.

Anyway, how hard could it be? I thought. I wouldn't even need lessons. I still had all the yellowing music books from the lessons I took as a child. It would be a breeze to whip through them and get up to speed. I'd be playing Mendelssohn's *Rondo Capriccioso* again in no time.

Wrong. I couldn't even master "Sister Sally's Seesaw." Obviously, I had to start from scratch, and I needed help. I decided to enroll in a highly recommended music school in the next town. I dutifully reported for my first lesson to the instructor assigned to me—a lady even older than I, with pince-nez glasses.

"Do you know how to read music?" she quavered. She was delighted when I said yes.

"Wonderful!" she trilled. "That will save a lot of time. Let me explain our system of sight reading to you," whereupon she unrolled a sheaf of paper decorated with gaudily colored birds perched on limbs resembling a musical staff.

"Here we go!" she said. "The canaries are eighth notes, the bluebirds are quarter notes, the green parakeets are half notes, and those big fat robins are whole notes. Now, let me see you try to play this lovely little song!"

Even if the big fat robins hadn't been in the process of eating big fat worms, I would have felt slightly ill. I peered at her. No, she wasn't kidding. She apparently had never taught anyone over the age of five.

"Do you suppose," I asked gently, "that we could try it with regular music? I think I could manage."

She couldn't have been more dismayed if I had proposed that she dye her hair shocking pink and pierce her bellybutton. "Heavens, no!" she said. "We couldn't possibly do that yet. That's not our system!"

I managed to refrain from telling her that I thought their system was for the birds, but I never went back for lesson two.

Instead, I checked out another music school in the area that had a marvelous reputation. It took only one lesson to realize why the school was, indeed, highly regarded—at least, in the financial community. Its prime focus was its bottom line, not the cultivation of its students' musical aptitude. An alarm clock was set at the beginning of a half-hour lesson, and the teacher raced against it through the whole session. When the time was up, the bell rang shrilly. The lesson was over. If a hapless student had a hand raised above the keys at that moment, ready to launch an intricate arpeggio, that arpeggio would remain unplayed until the next week's lesson.

I had paid for six weeks in advance in accordance with the school's play-it-safe terms, but my frazzled nerves couldn't take it any more after two.

I was ready to put an ad in the classifieds: "For sale, new spinet, barely touched by human hands." But I knew my skeptical pals were itching to unleash their smug I-told-you-sos. I couldn't give them that satisfaction. At least not yet.

As I pondered what to do next, my phone rang. A friend who had recently returned from a long trip had just heard about the funny things that had happened to me on my way to Carnegie Hall. "Your search is over!" she said. "I know a terrific teacher who specializes in adults. What's more, he doesn't know how to tell time. You'll love him."

I did. He persuaded me to abandon my Mendelssohn aspirations, at least for the time being, and just have fun at the piano. But first I had to memorize something he called "chords." This was a whole new concept to me. During a decade and a half of piano lessons in my first childhood, I had never been taught that those groups of notes on top of each other were chords—and they had names!

He then gave me some "music" written in letters and numbers on paper ruled off in squares. At least it looked a bit more sophisticated than colored birds, but people who saw it invariably asked how I could play geometry on the piano.

Though it appeared strange, it was effective. In three weeks, I was doing so well my teacher figured I was ready for my debut.

"I can arrange for you to play at the opening of that new supermarket down the street," he said. "On second thought, maybe not. Too many fruits and vegetables handy for the amateur critics to throw. How about a cocktail lounge instead? You could start late in the evening when the customers are so mellow anything will sound good."

When I accused him of not having any faith in my musical

ability, he said, "Not true. A few more lessons, and you'll be a pro. Stick with me, kid; I need the money."

Well, I did stick with him for another year or so; and I really did have fun with it, as he had advised me at the outset. But when I stopped taking lessons, I stopped playing. And, again, my musical neurons stopped functioning. Another example of the truth of the caveat, "Use it or lose it."

I'm now back where I began—wondering how in the world I had ever played "Sister Sally's Seesaw."

It's time for a new hobby.

Hey! Maybe I can go on E-bay and swap my neglected spinet for a bungee cord.

A Coward's Lament

As a child I was excruciatingly shy and timid. But I tried not to let it bother me because I was sure that when I grew up, I would magically become supremely self-confident. I guess I secretly believed that on the eve of my eighteenth birthday, Tinker Bell would leave a gift-wrapped assortment of poise, assurance, and savoir-faire under my pillow. But I blew it. I twisted a neck muscle that day so slept without a pillow. No pillow, no package from Tinker Bell. As a result, the silliest things can still intimidate me, such as . . .

Walking through the cosmetics aisles of a department store where hordes of glamorous, highly painted saleswomen block every path, spray me with their newest fragrances, and recommend various beauty potions and creams. Suddenly I'm painfully aware of my every flaw, blemish, and imperfection. Now convinced that I am hideous, how can I spurn the remedies they suggest? Anxious to appease them and escape, I relinquish my credit card and order one of everything. But does that satisfy them? Oh, no. They insist on demonstrating how the products should be applied. They plunk me down on a high stool and slather on their miraculous foundations, eye shadows, concealers, blushers, and lip glosses, as two dozen complete strangers gather around to watch. My worst nightmare! I'm a gawky fourteen-year-old again, and the homecoming queen and her court are snickering at me.

I'm also intimidated by anyone in a uniform, including kids in baseball suits collecting for the Little League at the supermarket entrance. Why in the name of Lou Gehrig aren't they out playing baseball instead of begging in the streets? And since I feel this way, why do I always make a donation when I enter the store? And why do I feel so guilty when I don't put another dollar in the can the same kid thrusts at me on my way out of the store? Especially since I don't have a dollar when I leave anyway.

Uniforms alone are bad enough, but show me a uniform plus a badge and I'll show you a blithering idiot. No, no! Not the person wearing the uniform and the badge—*me*. I see a policeman fifty feet away, and I'm ready to confess to anything. I'm sure I must have been driving twenty-one miles per hour in a twenty-mile-per-hour zone . . . I was jaywalking in my driveway . . . someone reported me for going through the six-items-or-fewer express checkout lane with a six-pack of Milky Ways and a package of gum . . . or I had an amnesia attack during which I gunned down thirty-seven people. Just read me my rights, officer, and I'll go quietly.

I also find uniformed Girl Scouts daunting. I'm really tired of that humdrum assortment of cookies they come around with every year, but do I tell that to the little girl in green? Of course not. I tell her I love them all, and I buy two boxes of each. Worse yet, over the next couple of weeks I stuff every last one into my mouth, even though I don't like them, and they're not on my low-carb diet. It's bad enough to be intimidated by a Girl Scout, but to be bullied by her cookies once she has left is really stupid. Why don't I simply throw them away? Because to waste food is a sin. (Oh, yes, God pushes me around, too.)

But it's not just the Almighty, uniforms, and inanimate cookies that intimidate me. I've also been known to cower before large dogs, Chihuahuas, and an occasional parakeet (caged).

Hairdressers have this strange effect on me, too. I always feel so vulnerable with my hair soaking wet. And it doesn't help to have a haughty, perfectly groomed stylist toss his luxurious mane in disbelief as he tsk-tsks about the terrible condition of my hair. When he informs me accusingly that it's dying (in fact, it may be too late—it's probably already dead), I feel like an unfit mother. I'm so ashamed I can't possibly refuse his suggested costly conditioners and special-formula shampoo (the price of which makes the conditioners seem like a bargain). When he finishes styling my hair, it actually looks worse than it did soaking wet, but I smile and gush, "That's great! Thanks!" and rush home to rewash and restyle my disastrous "do" before I run into anyone I know.

Which reminds me—I'm also demoralized by friends I bump into whenever I dash out for just a minute without makeup and in my grungy jeans to buy a quart of milk. They're all waiting for me—in the parking lot, by the dairy counter, at the checkout register. . . . And, of course, they all look fantastic.

Speaking of looking good, women whose tresses are long, straight, and blonde are one of my bugaboos. I just know they dated the captain of the football team from middle school through college, they sweet-talk their way out of speeding tickets, they never buy Girl Scout cookies, and they look so good with their hair soaking wet no one would dream of suggesting that they need special conditioners and shampoos.

I'm also reduced to a quivering mass of insecurity by men who are prettier than me, pushy car dealers, and drunks who misdial and wake me at three in the morning. I actually apologize to them because I'm not the person they're trying to reach.

But this worm is going to turn. I went to the library yesterday to get a book on how to be more aggressive. Unfortunately, they were all out. I'm on the waiting list—after the Little League fundraisers, the local police force, the hairstylists' union, Girl Scout troops 1 through 38, and the entire sales staffs of Macy's and Bloomingdale's. It's not fair. They don't need any help. *I* do!

I was going to ask the librarian to put me at the top of the waiting list, but I didn't dare. Librarians have always intimidated me.

Free at Last!

I don't know about you, but I for one am getting fed up with anecdotes about feisty folks from seventy to one hundred-plus who are working full time and never even take a vacation, except maybe a couple of days a year to visit their parents who are still punching the old time clock or plowing the back forty and hand milking their two hundred cows every dawn.

These poor misguided workaholics plan never to slow down. They'd have us believe that retirement is fatal, more dangerous than pirouetting blindfolded across the Grand Canyon on a tightrope. They swear that hard work is keeping them alive. Give me a break. That's living?

If they want to toil until the life supports are disconnected, fine. But must they keep preaching the work ethic and trying to make the rest of us believe that we're lazy, unproductive, and completely worthless because we feel we've earned the right to sleep in until 7:30 once in a while and maybe paint a picture, read a book, stitch a quilt, or catch a midweek theater matinee? Are we depraved because we revel in the freedom of being able to do our laundry, shop for groceries, clean our houses, or maybe even go to the beach on Wednesday instead of Saturday or Sunday, if we feel like it? Are we hopeless degenerates because we prefer Scrabble or bridge to the no-win game of company politics?

When I finally retired a while back, my boss (who had

relentlessly tried to talk me out of it) predicted direly that I would rue my rash decision. "You're going to just hang around the house all day in your bathrobe," he said. "Really?" I replied. "That sounds wonderful!" I have yet to do that; but it's so blissful to know that if I want to, I can. However, for the time being, I have too much to do.

How I ever found the time to work is a mystery to me. On the other hand, what I do all day is equally mystifying. People, including my aforementioned ex-boss, ask, "So what have you been up to?" I'm embarrassed to admit that I'm not exactly sure. I just know that I'm constantly busy. I haven't even had time to pick up the wonderful books I've been dying to read that my former workmates gave me at my retirement party (along with a gorgeous robe to "hang around" in). Nor have I yet managed to shorten the long list of people I promised to meet for lunch "some day soon."

No, I have not become a TV soaps addict. For all I know—or care—All My Children could have run away to Another World or be languishing in General Hospital hopelessly addicted to drugs As the World Turns. Okay, so I am familiar with the names of these epics, but that's just because I read the TV listings to be sure I'm not missing anything good. Obviously I'm not.

I'd like to say that my house is much cleaner these days, but who has time to dust and vacuum? I'm also ashamed to admit that though I was looking forward to finally doing some serious writing, this frivolous rambling is all I've managed to accomplish so far. I did start to keep a journal, just to have a record of how I was spending my time; but I gave that up very soon. It was too much like work—something I felt I "had to do" every day. Hey, I retired to escape the have-to's. Why manufacture new ones?

For now, I'm content to dabble. I enrolled in an Italian class, which I loved but never seemed to have the time to do the homework. I also took a course in watercolor—a real challenge considering I hadn't held a paintbrush since Kindergarten Art 101. I loved it. I, who always considered myself a "morning" person, actually found myself painting past midnight last week. No problem. I knew my alarm wasn't going to blast me out of bed at dawn to play traffic roulette on the turnpike. Such a luxury!

Every once in a while, I think I should feel guilty about not working. When that happens, I simply call some friends who are still enslaved and ask them how things are going. They tell me. Suddenly I'm cured.

I try very hard not to gloat.

Insomnia: More Hazardous Than You Think

Anyone who spends night after restless night tensely trying to fall asleep has heard all the advice: Don't eat a heavy dinner. Avoid caffeine. No late-evening exercise. Relax and unwind before going to bed. Once tucked in, if you're not asleep within twenty minutes, get up and go to another room. Read something boring, sip a glass of warm milk, count your blessings, count some sheep, but don't count your money (unless your name is Bill Gates or you've recently won the lottery). And above all, *don't* turn on the TV (unless your name is Bill Gates or you've recently won the lottery) because not only will it keep you awake, it will keep you broke.

Think about it. The pickings are slim at 2:00 A.M.; so as you channel surf, you're in great danger of being sucked into watching a home shopping show or a product infomercial. Bad. You're exhausted; your defenses are down; you're vulnerable. And, unfortunately, your phone and credit card are handy. This is a recipe for disaster. Take it from me.

During my many sleepless nights, I have purchased a variety of products that I'm certain my daytime self would have resisted—in fact, would often have ridiculed—including three food choppers. Why three? you may ask. Because No. 1 mangled instead of chopped, and No. 2 chopped adequately but required an advanced engineering degree to figure out how to disassemble it for cleaning. I was sure No. 3, a simple two-piece job that performed beautifully on camera, was my dream chopper. It turned out to be a nightmare. (It suddenly occurs to me that someone who yearns for a "dream chopper" needs to get a life.)

My next disastrous nocturnal purchase was a treadmill. It's bad enough to buy a treadmill without trying it out. But worse, because of my semi-somnolent state during the demonstrator's pitch, I did not heed three of the most dreaded words in the English language: "Some Assembly Required." The contraption arrived in seventeen pieces, plus a plastic bag containing forty-seven screws in various sizes, twenty-one bolts, eighteen wing nuts, fifty-five washers, and an illegible teeny-tiny assembly diagram. And I still didn't have that advanced engineering degree. It was marginally cheaper to return the whole mess than to enroll at MIT.

These experiences cooled my predawn impulse buying, but only temporarily. I'm embarrassed to disclose my other follies. I'll just say that they included some (though, thankfully, not all) of the following:

- Diet pills guaranteed to burn off a gazillion calories.
- Torso trimmers, thigh toners, tummy tamers, tush tighteners.
- Exercise videos, including one (I swear) that simply demonstrates walking.
- Hair-growing products.
- Hair-removal products.
- Wrinkle creams that promise to make Grandma Moses (even though she's dead) look like airbrushed photos of a twenty-year-old Elizabeth Taylor.
- A diamond ring the size of the one Richard gave the afore-mentioned once-lovely Liz. And such a bargain! (Call now! Only nine left!)
- A portable oven that cooks frozen foods faster than a microwave. (Why?)
- Food processors, dehydrators, juicers.

• A magnetic bracelet that miraculously abolishes all aches and pains. (Cheaper than a trip to Lourdes, and no need to update your passport.)

• An air purifier that annihilates pollen, animal dander, and millions of invisible dust mites as horrifying as Godzilla (have you seen those pictures?!) that have supposedly infested your bedding and everything else in your home.

Where are you going to find room for all these products? you might ask. Easy. Once you get rid of all those dust mites, you'll have ample space.

These are just a sampling of the offerings on late-night TV. All are extolled by an enthusiastic, glib demonstrator in front of an audience that obviously has been prepped to applaud wildly and "Oooh!" "Aaah!" or "Gasp!" at appropriate intervals. And all the products are available for a limited time at an "incredible" price, always preceded by "just" and "only," as in: "This amazing gizmo/doohickey/thingamabob can be yours for *just* four easy payments of *only* $999 each!" Plus shipping and handling, of course—a charge which in many cases could cover the cost of mailing the iceberg that sank the *Titanic*. And if you order within the next thirty minutes (i.e., before you wake up enough to realize what an idiot you are), they will include an ice crusher to reduce that iceberg to manageable chunks for your next cocktail party.

Okay, so I may have succumbed to some of this hype, but I'm not completely hopeless. One unique product I passed up was a train alarm clock consisting of a miniature town complete with trees, buildings, and people. At the preset wakeup time, the train rumbles through the town, engines chugging, whistles whistling, and bells ringing. I can't say I wasn't tempted. However, I had shredded all my credit cards during a rare fit of sanity a few minutes before the ad aired.

But I'm afraid I was too impulsive. How can I get along without a credit card? Well, I'll worry about that tomorrow. I really should turn off the TV now and try to get some sleep. No! Wait! They're just announcing a phone number I can call to get a new credit card that offers an interest rate of *only* 39 percent! And if I act immediately, I'll get a free trip to Timbuktu. All I'll have to pay for is hotel, food, ground transportation, and sightseeing (which shouldn't cost much—how many sights are there to see in Timbuktu?). And, oh yes, there is a small supplemental charge for airfare if I actually want a seat instead of joining my carry-on in the overhead rack.

What a deal! Gotta call right away!

It Was Here a Minute Ago

Most people have time to watch TV, read trashy novels, meander through malls, gossip on the phone, nap, daydream. . . . Not me. I can't indulge in such frivolous pursuits. I'm too busy looking for things I've misplaced.

In the time I've spent searching for lost keys, missing glasses, my pearl earrings, or my favorite chili recipe, I could have written one of those trashy novels other people find time to read. Instead, I can only dash off this short essay—which is a real exercise in futility since I won't have time to send it to my publisher. I'll be too busy looking for something. Like my car.

Yes, my car. I'm always losing it—on city streets, in parking lots, and once in front of my own house. I used to rent a garage from the neighbors across the street, you see. One night I came home late, and instead of driving into the garage, I parked smack up against a stairway that leads up an embankment to my house. The next morning, a slave to habit, I headed for the garage. No car. It must have been stolen! I rushed back across the street to call the police, but something stopped me. My car. It was blocking the stairs. I had actually had to squeeze past it a few minutes earlier when I went to the garage.

I thought no one could ever top that. But, of course, someone did. At church last Sunday the priest's homily concerned memory lapses. He told about a friend who had driven to Canada for a vacation. After a few days, he flew home—and promptly reported his car stolen because it wasn't there.

I know my "stolen" car story is true. It happened to me. But this parable from the pulpit is hard to believe. Still, would a priest make something up? Sure. Some have done worse. And some even write trashy novels. (Sorry, Father Greeley.)

I'm walking on thin ice here. I don't want to hurt any feelings in high places. I rely on people at the top, mainly Saint Anthony and Saint Jude, when I'm really desperate to find something. Scoff if you will. Whenever I ask, they always come through and lead me directly to whatever had been missing.

So what's my problem? Why do I spend hours searching for misplaced miscellany? Why don't I just call on Tony or Jude at the outset? Because I feel guilty diverting them from more important matters, like listening to all those people begging for help in finding a cure for cancer, world peace, lost hope. . . .

By comparison, locating that travel-size bottle of shampoo that I bought for my last trip, for example, is ridiculously trivial. I sure would like to know what happened to it, though. I clearly remember taking it out of the shopping bag and putting it on my bed, along with everything else I was packing. Then, somehow, it disappeared. I stripped the bed. I checked the floor around the bed, under the bed, even the bedsprings. That was six months ago, and it hasn't turned up yet. Not a trace. Maybe the dog stole it. But if she did, she never used it; she still looks grungy. Baffling.

It's not surprising that, when describing me, people often use the phrase, "She's lost it." They're right. In more ways than one.

Where Are You When We Need You, Cary Grant?

I love the movies. Actually, that's not really true. I *used* to love them. But not much anymore.

I'm sure it's because 99 percent of today's films are formulated to appeal to the younger generation—or, rather, to their grandchildren. From my perspective, you see, the "younger generation" is between forty and sixty, and the demographic audience targeted by today's moviemakers are the ten- to twenty-year-olds. Why? Because the concession stand, not the ticket revenue, supports the theater; and the kids are the ones who think nothing of shelling out large portions of their allowances or salaries from their part-time jobs for industrial buckets of popcorn swimming in fake melted butter, obscenely oversized candy bars, and half-gallon soft drinks. We older folks, whose wallets, tummies, and bladders can't withstand such fare, either do without nibbles at the movies or we sneak in a bag of microwaved popcorn or some supermarket chocolate Halloween goblins or Valentine hearts discounted after the holidays. At least, that's what I hear. Not me, of course. I never break the rule of "no outside food." (If my local theater manager is reading this, please be assured that the large purse I'm lugging contains only my knitting and a cough drop or two.)

It's not surprising, then, that since the teens and preteens are the big spenders, they're the ones calling the movie camera shots. Consequently, though many multiplexes feature over thirty different films, it's often impossible to find even one that appeals, unless you're into blood and gore; high-speed car chases; ear-splitting, eye-straining, nausea-inducing special effects; grotesquely muscle bound superheroes and impossibly bosomy heroines; or crude, vulgar slapstick.

Whatever happened to the tender love stories, intriguing mysteries, toe-tapping musicals, and sophisticated comedies of yore? Where are you when we need you, Cary Grant, Joan Fontaine, Jack Lemmon, Katherine Hepburn, Judy Garland, Jimmy Stewart, Grace Kelly, Clark Gable . . . and all the other glittering stars of the golden age of cinema?

We really appreciated the movies back then because they offered a glamorous escape from our relatively humdrum lives (oh, those gorgeous clothes . . . the magnificent mansions . . . the witty repartee!). We treasured every moment of each film because we knew we would get to see it only once, unless we could afford the fifteen-cent price to see it again in the next few days—a highly unlikely extravagance in that post-depression era.

Each town usually had just one theater (a single-screener) that showed one double feature per week—a major attraction with two stars of the day in the leading roles and a "B" picture with lesser luminaries, preceded by a newsreel plus a serial, such as *The Perils of Pauline,* which always ended with the heroine in a precarious situation (such as tied to the railroad tracks with a train fast approaching) to ensure we'd go back next week to see if she escaped. Such lures were not necessary, however. We would have returned regardless of our concern for Pauline. We eagerly anticipated each new picture; and when it arrived at the local ornate movie palace, we often stood in line for an hour or more to get in. After a few days, it would be gone forever—no TV runs, no videotapes, and no DVDs. We could revisit our favorite movies only in our memories, and many of them we never forgot.

Not so today's movies, too many of which are eminently forgettable, despite what the critics say. If you believe the reviews and the promotional hype, you'll have a very hard time choosing which film to see on any given day. In yesterday's newspaper, for example, the following blurbs appeared in ads for eight different movies:

THE BEST FAMILY FILM SO FAR THIS YEAR

THE BEST FILM OF THE YEAR

ONE OF THE FUNNIEST AND MOST
EXHILARATING MOVIES OF THE YEAR

THE MOST REMARKABLE MOVIE
YOU'LL SEE THIS YEAR

THE FILM AMERICA'S CRITICS ARE CALLING ONE OF
THE YEAR'S BEST

THE MOST ORIGINAL FILM THIS YEAR

ONE OF THE DEEPEST, MOST RIGOROUS, AND MOST
REWARDING FILMS OF THE YEAR

THE BEST THRILLER OF THE YEAR

In addition to the above, all of which, as you can see, proclaim superlatives for the year, many ads made other extravagant claims not related to any timeframe.

So how does one choose from such a lineup?

It's not really that difficult. I, personally, have found a formula that usually works for me: if the critics love it, I will probably hate it. For example, I saw a movie last week that was four-star rated. I, too, might give it four stars—on a scale of one to 100—but definitely not on the one-to-four scale the reviewer used.

There can be only one explanation for such a disparity of opinion. One of us has no taste whatsoever, and the other is a brilliant, discerning connoisseur of the arts.

What I don't understand is how come I'm not the one raking in a six-figure salary with my own movie-review TV show.

And the Oscar Goes To . . .

Do you watch the Academy Awards shows? Quite a spectacle with all the Hollywood VIPs and wannabes in their pricey designer gowns, tuxes, and ostentatious bling-bling strutting down the red carpet to the opulent Pantages Theatre, settling into their plush seats, and breathlessly waiting to learn if they will win a coveted Oscar—or if, instead, they will be forced to smile good-naturedly on camera and applaud a rival who has beaten them out. Win or lose, all the nominees at least have their moment in the spotlight.

But what about the rest of us? How come we don't get public acknowledgment for our achievements? Don't we deserve an award? Since it would admittedly be less significant than the Oscar, we could call it the Oscarette. It would be smaller than its illustrious namesake and made of plastic; but, hey, it would be better than nothing, right?

I can see it now: me in my fluorescent Wal-Mart creation (complemented by my Payless flip-flops and Dollar Store jewelry) sitting at a table at I-Hop with my fellow nominees, waiting to learn who will get the Oscarette for (drum roll, please) making the bed every morning before leaving the house.

My competition is stiff—my cousin Mary, who dusts and vacuums every inch of her home every single day; my neighbor Jean, a former nun, who trained in housekeeping for eighteen years under the demanding tutelage of Sister Agnes Frances, a name feared in all of conventdom; and my aunt Philomena, who is required by law to keep sunglasses on a table by her front door for guests lest they be permanently blinded by the spotlessness within.

I am choked with emotion. It is truly an honor just to be nominated among such illustrious company. If I am lucky enough to win, I hope I will not forget to thank all the little people who helped me along the way.

Oscarettes could be created for dozens of categories, including:

Closet cleaning: Someone who goes through his or her wardrobe and actually gets rid of some stuff certainly deserves an award. This prize may go unclaimed, however, since I, for one, have never heard of anyone ever doing this.

Courage to face the world, even on bad hair days: Since celebrities would not be eligible to be nominated for an Oscarette, Donald Trump would be prohibited from competing, leaving the field wide open for the rest of us.

Balancing your checkbook every month: A monumental achievement that undeniably deserves recognition.

Saving—and eventually also eating—leftovers: Simply storing them in the fridge for a few weeks and then discarding them disqualifies any candidate, which narrows the field considerably.

Not throwing your computer out the window when it crashes and destroys five years of work: Certainly such restraint merits a reward.

Cheerfully sharing the remote and all household duties with your spouse: Since this is a category for husbands only, there may never be a winner.

Answering your phone when your caller ID reveals the name of someone you'd like to avoid: This could be classified as a humanitarian award.

Resisting the urge to play computer solitaire instead of working: To be awarded by the winner's boss, along with a thank-you check of $50,000.

Leaving a note for the person whose car you scratched in the parking lot, even if no one saw you: A Ripley's Believe It or Not contender.

Reading your child her favorite bedtime story every night: Also known as the "I'm so sick of *Goodnight Moon* I could vomit!" Oscarette.

Other unsung heroes and heroines to be honored include those who exercise every day and pass up that second piece of cheesecake . . . limit their TV viewing only to PBS cultural offerings . . . declare every penny of income, documented or not, on their tax returns . . . make their own coffee every morning and donate to charity the three dollars they would have spent at Starbucks . . . floss every single night . . . don't sneak into the eight-items-or-fewer express checkout lane with nine items . . . don't pretend to be young by refusing all senior discounts . . . and many more.

The list of categories is interminable—just like the Academy Awards. Come to think of it, a special Oscarette should go to anyone who can stay awake for the entire Oscar show.

What do you think? Wouldn't we all go out there and tackle our everyday, humdrum lives with new enthusiasm, knowing we have an opportunity to someday hear those magical words: "And the Oscarette goes to . . . *you*"?

Oops! Look at the time! If I don't leave right now, I'm going to be late for my dentist appointment. But first I have to make the bed. Don't want to jeopardize my nomination.

Traveling Light

Hamlet had it easy. All he had to figure out was whether "to be or not to be"—a onetime dilemma, at least if he chose "not to be."

My own quandary, though admittedly relatively frivolous, is a puzzlement that challenges me whenever I plan a trip. My soul-searching question, which I am compelled to ask of every item in my closets and drawers, is "to pack or not to pack?" You'd think that it would get easier every time. Wrong. If anything, it seems to get harder.

Though I travel fairly frequently, I still haven't figured out what to take with me. I can be certain of only two things: if I leave it home, I'll wish I had it; if I pack it, I'll wish I hadn't.

The pioneers who crossed the Great Plains were lucky. They could cram all their stuff into the old Conestoga wagon. Come to think of it, they didn't have much stuff, as opposed to their wealthy descendants who crossed the Atlantic on luxury liners who did have a lot of stuff but didn't have a packing problem. They simply had their personal maids transfer the contents of their closets and chests to spacious steamer trunks.

Today most of us also have lots of stuff, but no personal maids; and we usually travel long distances on airships instead of steamships. Goodbye steamer trunk, hello dilemma.

The urge to overpack must be in our genes. It's hard to stifle.

If only we could remember that last trip when we had to schlep those heavy bags from home to the departure airport, from the arrival airport to the hotel—or, in the case of a multi-destination trip, to and from many hotels—the ultimate nightmare. Worse yet, unpacking at each stop along the way can consume hours that should be spent seeing the sights and mingling with the locals. Be honest. Wouldn't you rather be floating on a gondola while Giuseppe serenades you?

Maybe you think you can avoid the problem by not unpacking at all. Big mistake. Each time you dig into the recesses of your bulging bag searching for a pair of panties, your walking shoes, or your toothbrush, you anger the contents. They take on a life of their own, intertwining with and mangling each other, so that before long any semblance of order is destroyed and it is impossible to find anything.

I admire my friend Janet, who can go away for a month with one small carry-on bag and yet always look lovely. She follows all the expert advice and confines her travel wardrobe to a simple color palette so that one set of accessories coordinates with everything. She plans and packs so efficiently that on her last trip to attend a family wedding, she decided not to take the lovely lightweight silk dress she had planned to wear. Why? Because it had shoulder pads, and they'd take up too much room. The dress stayed home, replaced by an even lighter, padless creation.

Another friend, Joanne, on the other hand, wailed for days before our last Florida jaunt that she had to find time to go shopping before we left because she had absolutely nothing to wear. As it turned out, she didn't have time and didn't go shopping. Imagine my astonishment, therefore, when she showed up at the airport lugging three huge bags stuffed full of "nothing to wear."

It's not surprising that Joanne's favorite mode of travel is by automobile—preferably her own car (which is almost as big as a Conestoga wagon). Its huge trunk and roomy backseat can accommodate most of what she must take with her just in case—just in case it rains, just in case it snows, just in case there's a record-breaking heat wave, just in case it's freezing, just in case she's invited to several dressy affairs, just in case a gross of T-shirts and two dozen pairs of slacks and shorts won't be enough to get her through a week of casual outings. . . . Come to think of it, Joanne packs for a trip the way she shops for groceries. Her pantry shelves and refrigerator are always bulging with every imaginable treat favored by any friend who might possibly drop in—just in case.

It's surprising that she doesn't also tote a giant cooler crammed with goodies when she travels—just in case the meal service on the plane is slow and her fellow passengers might crave a tasty snack to tide them over.

It's a blessing that we can't take anything with us when we depart on our final journey. Can you imagine the dilemma of trying to decide what we'd need to get us through eternity?

How I Found God in Limbo-Land

On a trip to Bermuda a couple of decades ago, I learned the Good News. Religion lives! This revelation did not come to me in a quiet church on a tranquil lane, nor in a lush meadow carpeted with violets, nor by the incredible sea painted a brilliant turquoise only God could have wrought. No, I discovered religion in the function room and cocktail lounge of a luxury resort hotel where Evangelists gathered to bear witness to their faith.

No sackcloth and hair shirts for these worshippers. They wore instead crinolines, Western shirts, jogging shorts, or warm-up suits. For some of them were square dancers, and some of them were long-distance runners. And all of them had seen the light and were reborn.

They had come to that tiny isle in the mid-Atlantic on separate pilgrimages—one hundred square dancers from the United States for a weeklong festival for the Deity of Do-Si-Do, and a thousand runners from all over the world for a ten-kilometer offering of pain to whatever gods look after masochists in Nikes. And both groups were seeking converts with a fervor not seen since John the Baptist walked the earth. No one was safe from their proselytizing.

Not even me, an unwary vacationer looking for the cocktail lounge. Making a wrong turn, I suddenly found myself in Crinoline Country, surrounded by gray-haired matrons in short, flouncy, little-girl skirts and portly gentlemen in incongruous Levis and cowboy boots. I knew how Alice must have felt when she tumbled headlong into Wonderland. I turned to leave, explaining that I was lost. It was an unfortunate choice of words. Even a nonbeliever like me could mend my ways and share in the Eternal Joy, they said, urging me to sit down and watch the services.

They squared their sets, swung their partners, and moved through intricate patterns with studied symmetry and precision. Their faces were furrowed in painful concentration as they performed one maneuver while straining to hear the caller's next command. This is fun?

"Oh, yes, indeed!" they exclaimed. "You'll see!"

It sounded like a threat. A chill ran through me as helpful fingers flicked through pocket directories until they found a square dance group in my hometown. An acolyte was instructed to phone and enroll me immediately.

"No!" I protested. How could I tell them that puffy petticoats and Mary-Jane slippers would destroy the sophisticated Cosmogirl image I'd been striving for? "I wouldn't fit in," I said, trying to sound unworthy.

"Nonsense!" they countered. "Everyone fits in. Doesn't matter if you're a Supreme Court judge or a garbage collector!"

"Worse luck," said I, trying to sound disappointed. "I'm neither."

It didn't work. They were still determined to baptize me into the fold. And catechism instruction began immediately. "We have only two commandments," they said. "Thou shalt not drink alcoholic beverages before a dance lest thy step falter; and thou shalt use lots of deodorant lest ye offend thy partners."

Here was my out. I scurried through. "I have a confession," I said. They bent forward, ready to forgive. "I have a perspiration problem that's so bad, it drives me to drink." After a moment of shocked, sympathetic silence, they made a very wide path to let me pass.

I resumed my search for the cocktail lounge. This time I found it. But something was wrong. It smelled like a locker room after the big game. Obviously, there were no deodorant-addicted square dancers here. However, again too late, I realized I had unwittingly crashed yet another gathering of zealots. The lounge was jammed with runners rigorously training for the Bermuda 10K to be held the following day. This phase of their regimen consisted of chug-a-lugging huge mugs of beer and swallowing fistfuls of peanuts and pretzels. At the center of this strange communion service, surrounded by adoring believers, was the aging guru of long-distance runners, Dr. George Sheehan, who has long since passed on and I'm sure is now running marathons in Heaven. But back then, in that little bit of Paradise on earth, he was expounding on the glories of physical fitness, the benefits of strenuous exercise. He looked awful—gaunt, green, and gasping for breath—as he exhorted all to go forth and exhaust themselves, to hurl themselves gladly against the "wall of pain" where thousands of marathon martyrs before them had been sacrificed.

"Why, o Wise One?" I asked, seeking to comprehend the great mystery.

"Because," he intoned, "unless you go through suffering and guilt and death, you miss the initiation."

I had no idea what in God's name he was talking about. I just knew it sounded like no fun at all, and I decided the only running I was going to do was away from there.

But, again, I was thwarted. The guru's disciples enfolded me, trying gentler persuasions. They told me of the high runners achieve, the joy, the oneness with the Universe. They spoke of other cynics before me who had scoffed at the Word and now gladly did ten miles of penance a day.

I pleaded advanced age. "No sweat!" they said. "Look at Dr. Sheehan."

"I did," I replied. "That poor man!"

They laughed, convinced I was joking. So I played my trump card. "I don't like to complain," I said. "But I have this trick knee. . . ."

"Come and meet Bobby," they said.

"Who?"

"Bob Hall. He was stricken with polio as a child, but that didn't stop *him*. He races in a wheelchair. He'll inspire you."

They led me to him. He was seated at a table with friends. When we approached, his companions rose to greet me. And then, miracle of miracles, so did Bobby! He walked towards me to shake my hand! That cocktail lounge was another Lourdes! "I believe! I believe!" I cried, falling on my knees in ecstasy.

It wasn't until the next day, when they were pinning a number on my back at the starting line, that I discovered that Bob had been walking for years. But he can take only a few steps at a time, and running is impossible. Hence the wheelchair for his racing. There had been no miraculous, spontaneous cure after all.

Here, then, was a true sign. God's way of telling me I'd been had. I ripped the number from my back as the starting gun went off, and I headed in the opposite direction.

"You're going the wrong way!" shouted runners streaming by me. But in my heart I knew I was finally on the Right Path— back to the hotel to join a new congregation that had checked in that morning—a group of Sun Worshippers who by now were basking on the beach. Now that's a religion I can live with.

Eeek! (Are We Having Fun Yet?)

Since when did defying death become enjoyable?

The roller coasters of my childhood were more than terrifying enough for me. I ventured on one only once, when I was in my teens, because I was tired of the gang calling me chicken. Actually, I'm embarrassed to admit that though that ride traumatized me for life, it wasn't even a real roller coaster. It was a scaled-down child's version called the Wild Mouse. When the passengers disembarked, five-year-olds were begging, "Again, Mommy, please!" as I staggered as far away from the beast as possible before losing my lunch. When I see today's coasters, with their ninety-degree vertical ascents and gravity-defying plunges, I don't know whether to be awestruck by the riders' courage or seek to have them committed to the nearest mental institution for their own protection. Think of it—one loose screw in the safety bar across the seat, or a glitch in whatever mysterious force keeps the cars on the rail, and it's all over. This is fun?

It's the same with hot-air balloonists. There they are, floating thousands of feet in the air in a flimsy wicker basket, next to a roaring flame that's licking yards of surrounding fabric—not to mention the explosive gas that feeds that flame. Yet they tell me it's beautiful. So peaceful. And at the end of the journey a soft landing in a green meadow awaits, followed by a celebratory champagne lunch. Maybe. Unless the air currents deposit them in the ocean . . . a traffic-congested highway . . . a cage full of lions at the local zoo . . .

Equally unappealing (at least to me) is the so-called thrill of parasailing. *I've* never tried it, of course. But once when I was on vacation I did see a crazy woman dangle from a parachute tethered to a speeding boat. Just watching was scary enough. One minute she was sailing blissfully through a brilliant blue sky, and the next (when the boat towing her took a sharp turn to avoid a jet skier), suddenly the parachute was whizzing dangerously close to shore, threatening to slam her into the penthouse suite of a luxury hotel at fifty miles an hour. No, thanks. I'll take the elevator. Of course, if you see in advance that you're getting too close to land, I suppose you could unhitch the chute and ditch into the water (provided that, unlike me, you can swim). But wait. Is that a school of sharks down there?

And what's with idiots who jump out of airplanes? I won't even descend a short flight of stairs without clutching the railing. No way would I hurl myself from a plane willingly. They would have to hire the Incredible Hulk to pry my hands loose from the doorframe and fling me out. And I'm sure I'd die of fright before I'd be able to pull the ripcord of the parachute. Or, more likely, I'd pull it the moment my feet touched air, and the chute would get ensnared in the plane's wings. Either way, it wouldn't be pretty.

Whitewater rafting is another sport I can live without (literally). I try to avoid even *still* water that's more than ankle deep. Do you think I'm going to climb into a little rubber boat and launch myself into a roiling river punctuated by boulders and tree limbs? Are you kidding?

Then there's bungee jumping. I ask you, can you really be sane and dive off a bridge, cliff, or tower trusting that a big rubber band is going to break your fall before you break your neck?

You have to be equally trusting to climb onto the back of a burro and allow it to carry you to the floor of the Grand Canyon, its hooves skirting the edges of precipices every inch of the way. It's perfectly safe, they tell us. These animals are amazingly surefooted. But are they telling us everything? Has one ever twisted an ankle or been spooked by a swarm of bees? I don't even want to contemplate the consequences.

Others far braver than I don't worry about such risks. Even as I write this, I'm sure someone is climbing the sheer wall of Half Dome at Yosemite, surfing the mountainous waves off Kauai, schussing down the Matterhorn, hang gliding over the Rockies. . . . The insanity is everywhere.

And me? I'm about to take a Valium so I can get up enough nerve to nuke my dinner. Those microwaves terrify me.

I Haven't a Thing to Wear

Three mysteries will always baffle me: Einstein's Theory of Relativity, how to buy low and sell high, and how it's possible to have three huge closets crammed with clothes and still never have a thing to wear—at least nothing appropriate for the occasion at hand.

Everything I own is either too formal or too casual for anything to which I'm ever invited. I seem to have an uncanny knack for either buying all the wrong clothes or not getting asked to any of the right affairs.

For instance, I was recently requested to attend a surprise anniversary party to be held at four o'clock on a Sunday afternoon. I was very smug as I slipped into my simple, elegantly tailored suit that the saleswoman had assured me would be at home at any afternoon social event. That's just where I should have left it—at home. When I arrived at the party, I had the feeling that the other women guests belonged to a secret sorority. All of them (including the lady being "surprised") knew something I didn't. There they were—every last one of them—dripping diamonds and black chiffon to their anklebones. At first I thought I had the wrong address and had stumbled into a very dressy wake. But nobody had died. I just wished I could.

However, uncomfortable though I was, I apparently wasn't considered completely disgraced, because a few weeks later someone in the same group sent me an elaborately engraved invitation to a garden party. Naturally, I didn't have a thing to wear, but they weren't going to fool me twice. This time the formality of the invitation gave me a clue as to what would be suitable. I went shopping and tried on one of the latest "in" fashions. I was positive it was "in" because no woman in her right mind would want to be seen "out" in it. But it was the mode of the moment, so I bought it. Before leaving for the party, I scrutinized myself in my full-length mirror and couldn't decide if I looked like a dress extra in a ball scene in a Victor Herbert operetta or a fugitive bridesmaid from a royal wedding. But I was absolutely certain of one thing—I was appropriately done up for a formal garden party. Unfortunately, the shindig turned out to be a backyard barbecue. Again, all the other sorority sisters knew. They were huddled around the spit in their cutoff denims and scruffy Adidases.

The following week, when another group of friends invited me to a cookout, I rushed out and bought some jeans, buried them in the garden overnight, soaked them in harsh detergent for three days, and then cut and frayed the cuffs. Perfect, I thought, as I jogged off to the cookout. I had even remembered to forget to put on makeup and comb my hair. You guessed it—the other guests were doing act 2 of *The Merry Widow* that evening. I was so embarrassed I beat a hasty retreat, pleading a terrible headache that had made it impossible for me to wear my tiara.

I'm really getting paranoid about this. How come everyone but me knows what to wear? I even felt like a misfit driving through the tollbooth on the Massachusetts Turnpike yesterday. I thought I was very chic in my designer T-shirt, leather skirt, thong sandals, and car, all in matching red. But wouldn't you know—all the toll collectors were wearing green.

I swear I wouldn't even know what to wear to a nude beach. I'd show up in a fig leaf and everyone else would be wearing violets and expressions that said, "My dear, don't you know that costume went out with Adam and Eve?"

I could really use one of those outfits they advertise that can "go anywhere" with a few deft changes of accessories. You've seen them at fashion shows. A snooty model slinks onto the runway in a precisely tailored pantsuit, "perfect for that important board meeting." When the meeting adjourns, Ms. Chic slips out of her slacks and into a matching wraparound skirt (which had been doubling as a headband), and voila! She's ready for lunch at the Four Seasons, after which her handsome escort takes her to a nearby exclusive beach club. Once there, she simply takes off everything—except the tropical-print bikini panties and bra that double as beachwear. After she enjoys a refreshing swim, her bathing suit and hair drip-dry to perfection in ninety seconds flat; and since her waterproof makeup hasn't so much as smudged, she's ready to dress and return to work. She arrives just as her phone rings. It's Prince Charming. He's picking her up at the office at six o'clock for a gala night on the town. What to wear? No problem. She simply doffs her blouse and bra and ties her chiffon handkerchief halter-style around her firm bosom. She then unzips her hem, releasing a floor-length flounce. A touch of Chanel, a hint of lip gloss, and she's off. And you just know that she and her smashing attire will be the page-one feature of *Women's Wear Daily* tomorrow.

I've just got to get me one of those outfits. On second thought, why? I don't need one. The only times I'd been asked to important board meetings were in my unliberated past when I carried in the coffee, and a simple apron and cap would have done nicely. And it's been months since anyone has invited me to the Four Seasons—or even McDonald's, for that matter. Furthermore, I can't swim, and I doubt if Prince Charming even has my phone number.

Besides, there's one big advantage to not having exactly the right thing to wear. It's a great excuse when you really don't want to accept an invitation. I'm planning to use it, in fact, when the Grim Reaper comes to fetch me. "Gee, I'm sorry," I'll say, "I can't possibly go—I haven't a thing to wear."

Where Is Ponce de Leon When I Need Him?

I remember when my darling mother was the same age I am now and I suggested she visit her local Senior Center. She was appalled. "Why would I want to spend time with all those old people?" she asked. I laughed. I'm not laughing anymore. I know exactly how she felt.

I have dropped into my Senior Center from time to time—for a computer class, a watercolor demonstration, an introduction to Tai Chi—but I always felt like an interloper. Sure, the activities are great, and the people there are all very nice to me; but I simply don't belong. I'm much too young. Maybe in ten years or so, I've been telling myself. But during one visit, I went into the ladies' room. Big mistake. They have mirrors in there.

It's just as bad when a movie ticket seller or a store clerk automatically gives me the senior discount. I love the bargain, of course; but how come they simply assume I qualify? I should have to ask for it, and they should be incredulous and demand to see some ID. I'm not unreasonable. I don't expect them to deny me entrance to an R-rated film because they think I'm too young, but neither should they automatically classify me as ancient.

When did this happen? Wasn't it only just last week that Hollywood actually made some movies suitable for children, and I used to get in for the child's price (ten cents, I think it was) . . . and the day before yesterday that I graduated from college . . . and yesterday that I was the youngest person at my first job? Now look at me. No, don't! Wait until I turn the lights down a bit.

When did I get old? I know when it all began—when I was a child, impatient to grow up. I couldn't wait to start kindergarten with the big kids . . . to go to junior high school (no middle schools back then) . . . to wear lipstick . . . to start dating . . . to go to high school . . . all the time wishing the months away until summer vacation. Then I wanted to be sixteen . . . get a car . . . go to college! And I was just as eager to graduate and start a career, assuming I'd be young forever—or at least for such a long time that it would no longer matter. Then, before I knew what hit me, I was young no more. And it mattered. Lots.

Sad to say, I never learned my lesson. Instead of trying to slow down the clock and enjoy the moment, I'm still impatient for future events. And my friends are no help at all. One of them, knowing I hate winter, keeps trying to cheer me up from November to March by saying, "Don't worry; it will be spring before you know it!" I could throttle her. Spring means another birthday for me.

But I'm not the only one experiencing the race of time. It's an epidemic. When, for example, did Burt Reynolds, Paul Newman, and Kirk Douglas go from being dreamboats to old wrecks? Not to mention those over-the-hill ladies masquerading as Mary Tyler Moore (who, like me, was the youngest person in her office), Elizabeth Taylor (that cute twelve-year-old in *National Velvet*), and June Allyson (the perpetual teenager). What's even scarier is that it won't be long before Cameron Diaz will no longer be cute and perky, and Matt Damon's smooth mug will begin to look like the roadmap that was once Robert Redford's gorgeous face.

The men, however, do seem to have a better deal. Look at Kirk's son, Michael, for instance. He gets to marry a beauty half his age, and few think it's strange. If I went after a boy toy, people would smile indulgently and have me committed to the nearest asylum. Which is okay. I wouldn't know what to do with him if I caught him anyway.

I can't help but wonder if Ponce de Leon ever actually found the fountain of youth. Could be that he did but has kept it a secret and is living in Miami picking up chicks at South Beach every night. I hope that with all that high living he doesn't exhaust the proceeds from his Explorers 'R Us pension plan before the fountain runs dry or the next condo developer plows it under.

If you're reading this, Ponce, take heed! Bottle as much of that water as you can and send it to a safe place—my house. If you won't do that, could you at least poll the grandmothers of the girls you're dating and ask them to recommend a good plastic surgeon who works cheap?

Lucky at Last!

I used to be one of those people who never win anything. But my luck finally has changed. Almost daily I receive at least one notification that I may have won a million-dollar dream house, a six-month around-the-world cruise in the *QE2*'s penthouse suite, a $100,000 Mercedes . . . it's mind boggling.

I did worry how I was going to pay the taxes on all these goodies, but I don't anymore, because yesterday I learned I'm a frontrunner for a million-dollar tax-free award! Hopefully, that will cover the tariff on my other prizes.

Even more amazing is the fact that all these riches are coming my way with little or no effort on my part. For example, just today I found out I'm tied for a $25,000 first prize in a word-puzzle contest that I had never even entered. How lucky is that? Accompanying the announcement of my good fortune was an offer to sell me—for a mere five bucks—a list of high-scoring words to help ensure my tie-breaking victory. Could I refuse to spend $5 to win a practically guaranteed $25,000? You betcha.

Another offer I found easy to decline was a "gemstone" I had won. To claim it I had to send only $5.95 to cover postage. But first I glanced through the company's catalogue that accompanied my prize announcement. Incredibly, it offered similar gemstones to the general public at $5.95, postage included.

Wouldn't you think they'd have been smart enough to at least mail the catalogue separately?

I also receive, at least once a week, scratch cards offering three possible prizes, ranging from paltry to priceless (or so they imply). I'm instructed to scratch the circle on the card to reveal which of these awards I'll win, simply by ordering a useless, overpriced thingamajig. Invariably, my circle reveals not only the top prize, but all three! What are the odds?

In addition, I have become a magnet for prestigious organizations, one of which recently wrote me, "Frankly, **MS. MULA**" (yes, bold capitals to make me feel important), "you're the type of successful person we want as a member of our exclusive club." Me? Successful? What great news! Enclosed with the letter was a list of several annual earnings ranges. I was supposed to check the one that applied to me. None did. In fact, my lifetime earnings to date don't match any of the annual earnings choices. Apparently their computers had mistaken me for some other **MS. MULA,** one who actually is successful. Since I was too embarrassed to admit that—and since I did not want to "invest" (their word) a thousand dollars to cover the admission dues—I declined the invitation to join their select society.

They must be devastated. I would have added a ton of class to the organization, because last week I received a postcard from the principality of Hutt River Province in the South Seas notifying me that I have been nominated for a Royal Award. It seems that their search through the Mula family tree found noble blood, indicating that I have "High Principles." The note promised me the same fame and fortune enjoyed by others who have received this Royal Award. Furthermore, His Royal Highness, the Prince Regent, Prince Kevin, would personally approve my award.

In order to claim this honor (of "incalculable value," they assured me), all I had to do was sign an Oath of Confirmation and return it, along with a statutory investiture fee of ten dollars. A bargain, right? Unfortunately, there was a catch. The Oath affirmed that I would not misuse or abuse the power and influence of my new Royal Award. Alas, since I truly do have High Principles, I could not in good conscience sign such an affirmation. After all, unaccustomed as I am to power and influence, how could I be sure it would not all go to my head and that, in the time it would take to say "Prince Kevin," I would be misusing and abusing my power and influence all over the place? I regretfully tore up my nomination.

Besides, I wouldn't have time to perform my royal duties. I'll be too busy pursuing the e-mail request from a high-ranking official in the Nigerian National Petroleum Corporation, who begged for my help since he had somehow learned (maybe from Prince Kevin?) that I am a reputable individual. He asked permission to secretly deposit into my bank account $50 million that the Nigerian government overpaid on a procurement contract. He is seeking a foreign haven in which to hide the money rather than returning it to the government. (Obviously his own principles are a bit questionable.) If I assist in this transfer by divulging my bank account information, he will pay me a commission of 30 percent, or $15 million. Since that sum would just about cover the cost of some periodontal work I need, I am sorely tempted. However, the plan requires me to travel to Nigeria immediately to complete the transaction, and there's no way I can leave town right now. I have been practically assured that I'm a winner of a $50 million lottery I entered (for a mere $10), but I have to be here to claim the prize in person.

Maybe you can help out the Nigerian. May I give him your bank account number?

Last One In's a Scaredy-Cat!

Recently I was talking to my grandniece, Shelley, about the many things I would do differently if those who believe in reincarnation are right and we get more than one shot at life. The big problem, though, I said, is that I probably won't remember them all. "Don't worry, Rosie," she replied. "If I know you, you'll have Post-It notes all over your casket."

Not a bad idea. And the largest note will say: *Learn to swim!* Actually, I *almost* learned to swim several years ago at an age when most people are taking up rock—the kind you do in a chair, not at a disco. I don't know why it took me so long. Apparently it goes back to my childhood, and, of course, my mother was to blame (or so the psychobabble says). Since she was afraid of the water and overprotective, she transmitted that fear to me.

At that time, many of our relatives lived on the shores of the icy Atlantic in Winthrop, Massachusetts, and my parents and I spent every summer weekend with them at the beach. All my cousins were as at home in the water as the ubiquitous minnows. They (the cousins and the minnows) obviously all had well-adjusted mothers.

Every weekend, cousins, aunts, and uncles—all well intentioned—would nobly try to help me overcome my abject terror of the deep (hey, it was up to my knees!) by trying to teach me to swim. They all invariably employed the same method. Each, in turn, would coax (spelled *d-r-a-g*) me, screaming, into the frigid water, force me over onto my stomach, and absolutely swear they would not let go of me. But they always did. And I would sink choking and panic stricken to the bottom—only eighteen inches down, but the bottom, nevertheless.

It got so I didn't like summers very much, especially weekends, until I grew older and stronger and adamantly refused to be dragged seaward anymore. My family finally abandoned their hopeless efforts and left me alone to splash happily in the shallow waters (where I pretended to be babysitting for any nearby toddlers so I wouldn't look too peculiar). Gradually I began to like summer weekends, the beach, and my relatives—in that order.

However, as the years went by, it became more and more embarrassing being the only one in the crowd who couldn't swim. At the seashore, I could get by with standing waist deep, pretending to tend the ever-present toddlers and jumping over the waves. At pools, however, since there was no surf, it was a different story. I'd sit in the sun, almost prostrated by the heat, looking longingly at the rest of the gang happily swimming in the cool, azure water. I'd have given anything just to get wet and cool off, but I knew I'd look foolish just standing or sitting in the shallow end, where even the tiniest tots were actually swimming. And since my friends knew I wasn't babysitting, that old ploy wouldn't work.

But even more uncomfortable than the heat were the inevitable questions. My old friends said nothing. They knew why I was dry-docked. But there were always some new ones who would naturally yell, "Hey, Ro! Aren't you coming in?" I was afraid an admission that I couldn't swim would result in an instant replay of my childhood beach outings—only worse. This time my instructors wouldn't be relatives; they'd be the few new boys we'd met that weekend whom we were all trying to impress.

Since I felt that even bone dry I wasn't all that impressive, I knew I wouldn't have a chance once they saw me choking and sputtering, with matted hair streaming over my fear-contorted face. So I'd be very vague about why I wasn't in the water. In those days, women didn't swim at "that time of the month," so the boys would soon redden and stop asking. (It didn't take much to embarrass boys back then.) It wasn't easy, and I always welcomed the first frost of the year.

But one winter shortly after I had graduated from college and had accumulated a few paychecks, I somehow got talked into a Miami Beach vacation with a couple of friends. I guess I was thinking of those star-filled nights, completely forgetting about the sun-drenched days. And there it was again—the bane of my existence—the dreaded swimming pool. As usual, I didn't dip even the tip of a toe into it. And since I couldn't cavort in the surf because great globs of jellyfish had staked a prior claim, I resigned myself once again to baking in the sun.

On the second day of our stay, a friendly young man with a cheerful grin walked up to where I (parched and dry) and my two friends (refreshingly wet from their recent dips) were sitting on our deck chairs.

"Hi!" he announced. "I'm Charlie. Is there anyone here who can't swim?"

I turned, pretending to scan our immediate neighbors for someone who qualified, hoping to draw attention away from myself. It almost worked, but my so-called friends ratted on me.

"She can't!" they squealed in unison, pointing at me.

Charlie was delighted. "Come!" he said, taking my arm. "I will teach you!"

"No, thank you," I said, trying to yank my arm free.

"Don't thank me—I'm looking for business," he said. "I'm the hotel's swimming instructor."

Great. I could get out of this one. I pleaded an extremely tight budget and told him that much as I'd like to learn to swim, I certainly couldn't afford professional lessons.

"It's only fifty dollars for the whole week, and I guarantee to teach you," he said.

"Sorry," I insisted. "Can't afford it." But my former friends turned into instant reverse Judases. Instead of accepting money to betray me, they actually shelled it out. Charlie beamed as he told me there was no limit to the lessons. He would simply spend as much time with me as necessary, even if it took eight hours a day for the rest of the week. And we would start right then, that very minute. Wonderful.

Little had I realized when I got up that morning that disaster was waiting for me fourteen flights down. Nothing I could do or say would dissuade him; so before I knew it, there I was, down by the pool. Looking up as I stood there, I had a good view of the two large sundecks surrounding the pool and everyone sitting there who had a wonderful view of me. And I was a sight to see.

By now, my teacher/tormenter had supplied me with a 1920s-style bathing cap, three sizes too big, which kept slipping down over my eyes and the bridge of my nose, which, in turn, was decorated with a lovely rubber nose plug. And on my feet, the piece de resistance—two huge swimming fins, which completed my transformation into a refugee from a Disney cartoon.

"Okay!" said Cheery Charlie. "We're going in the water now!"

Anything to get out of sight, at least partially; so I started following him—and fell flat on my face. I had never learned to walk with giant webbed feet. He helped me up, and I finally made my agonizing way into the pool (the shallow end, needless to say), where Charlie tried to get my feet off the bottom by promising he would hold me and not let go. Hah! I'd heard that song before. After an hour of fruitless effort, I hoped he was ready to forfeit his fee and give up—or even keep the money and give up. In fact, I'd pay him a bonus.

But I was a challenge, so he continued patiently until he finally won my confidence. And, miracle of miracles, by the end of the third hour, Charlie actually had me doing a very tense dead man's float. I was the stiffest stiff ever, but I was really floating! Dizzy with success, Charlie would not let me quit while we were both ahead. He instructed me to hold on to the ridge at the side of the pool and, hand over hand, work my way around to the deep end. The mere words "deep end" turned me to stone once more. Charlie stopped and picked up a long pole. "Look," he said, "even if you do sink, I can get you with this in seconds; you won't drown."

"I know," I said. "The heart attack would get me first."

I think he realized I wasn't kidding (and how would that look in the papers?), so he finally took pity on me and helped me out of the pool. I avoided it and him for the rest of the week.

After I had been home a few months, I read in the paper that the local Boys & Girls Club was offering beginner swimming lessons for adult women. I still remembered that frightening but glorious moment when I had actually floated (was it a dream?) and wondered if I could do it again. At any rate, it would at least be heartening to meet some other "adult women beginning swimmers."

The first evening there, the instructor (a mere slip of a nine-teen-year-old who looked as though she couldn't save a drowning Barbie doll) announced to a shivering bunch of women in the pool, "Okay—those of you who can keep afloat, go to the left side of the pool. The others stay here."

Since I had no confidence at all that I really could float, I decided I'd better be one of "the others." It turned out I was the only "other." As all the frauds who had claimed to be beginners floated gracefully away, the instructor said to me, "You stay here and practice until you can float. Then you can join us."

I tried. I really did. I tried to recall everything that Charlie had told me. I tried to pretend he was there to keep my head above water if I should start to sink. I tried to relax. I tried to figure out what in God's name I was doing there. I spent most of the remainder of the hour skinning my knees at the bottom of the pool, and I never went back for another so-called lesson.

But in my next incarnation, I'll show 'em! And while I'm at it, would you please hand me one more Post-It note? There's also this ice-skating thing, you see . . . and, oh yeah, skiing . . . and dancing . . . and singing . . . and tennis . . . and . . . oh, what the heck, you'd better give me the whole pad.

I Remember (II) Papa

Shortly after his election, Pope John Paul II visited Boston in 1979 and celebrated a televised Mass on the Common. The ceremonies caught the eye of my cousin's two-year-old daughter, Lauren, who had not turned off the TV in the family room after watching "Sesame Street." She was thunderstruck. She ran breathlessly into the kitchen exclaiming, "Mommy! Mommy! Uncle Jimmy's on TV in fancy clothes!"

It was a common mistake. For Lauren's uncle Jimmy—my dad—was a ringer for the pope. Except for the fancy clothes. A retired barber who had worked as a sulfur miner in Sicily when he was only eight to help support his family, he could never have afforded such a sumptuous wardrobe.

Nevertheless, the physical resemblance was uncanny—in spite of the fact that at the time, my dad was eighty—old enough to be the Holy Father's father.

Though many years have passed since John Paul II assumed the papacy and his picture appeared on the world's front pages, magazine covers, and television screens, I still clearly remember how my parents' phone rang continuously. Friends and relatives from coast to coast called to report the news. "Jimmy looks exactly like the pope!" they declared. "You've got it wrong," my mother corrected. "The pope looks exactly like Jimmy."

Whatever. My dad thoroughly enjoyed his celebrity status.

Wherever he went, people asked for his blessing—and he gave it. He had the hand movements down pat. He was sure God didn't mind.

Once a month he used to visit a local rest home (to give haircuts to the "old folks," he said, even though most of them were younger than he). They loved to see him come. "Here's the pope!" they'd announce. He smiled his beatific smile, blessing and snipping as he went.

On the street, strangers stopped him and said, "Oh, my God . . . !" "No, only Jimmy," replied my father.

At one point, he was in the hospital for minor surgery. One afternoon, people passing by to visit other patients were startled to hear a nurse call out to an orderly, "The pope needs a bedpan— room 316." As soon as he was out of bed, he made rounds with the hospital chaplain and reportedly boosted morale 100 percent.

Shortly thereafter, I entered my dad in a Boston television station's celebrity look-alike contest. "Be sure he comes in costume," they said. Those fancy clothes? There was no way we could duplicate them. So we settled for a long white alb borrowed from his parish pastor and a white yarmulke donated by a Jewish neighbor. A nice ecumenical touch. My mom supplied a four-inch crucifix to hang around his neck and I gave him a hefty costume-jeweled ring for his followers to kiss. We stood back to appraise him. Damned—I mean—darned if he didn't look even more like the pope than the pope himself! And darned if he didn't win first place, nosing out Alan Alda and Colonel Sanders (actually, reasonable facsimiles). The prize was a contract with Ron Smith's Celebrity Look-Alikes, a Los Angeles agency that supplies celebrity doubles for work in movies, television commercials, and print ads. My father was ready to pack his bags and hit the road. A whole new career! Fame! Fortune! He was ecstatic. Unfortunately, he was still waiting for his first assignment when he died three years later.

I wasn't surprised. Let's face it. The commercial opportunities for a pope look-alike are rather limited. I mean, they couldn't have him sipping a Beefeater martini in front of a blazing fire with a gorgeous blonde, kicking up his Doc Martins at a singles' disco, or riding the range with a Marlboro dangling from his lips. (Though the Marlboro man hadn't yet been banned from ads at that time, he would not have been an appropriate role model for His Holiness.)

But there were other possibilities. How about ice cream? What could be more wholesome than that? Picture this: my father, in full papal regalia (compliments of Baskin Robbins), licking an ice-cream cone, smacking his lips, and saying, "It's heavenly!" (So he would have said it in broken English; who would know it wasn't a Polish accent?)

Also, he could have been shown christening a Cabbage Patch Kid, which were ubiquitous back then, or officiating at Ken and Barbie's wedding, if those two ever decided to legalize their relationship.

Unfortunately, Ron Smith apparently wasn't able to sell any of these brilliant ideas, so Dad had to be satisfied with local personal-appearance requests that came his way. The most memorable was from my friend Carol, who was, and still is, famous for her extravagant parties. She called me when she was planning a wing-ding for her husband's fiftieth birthday. "Would your father like to play pope at my party?" she asked. "Is the pope Catholic?" I replied.

The big night arrived. Dad donned his alb, yarmulke, crucifix, and "papal" ring. Mom and I drove him to the party and sneaked him into a back room. The extravaganza reached a fever pitch. Finally, the guests were all seated for dinner. Suddenly there was a roll on the drums. The MC grabbed the microphone. "I'm sorry to delay your dinner, folks," he said, "but we've just received word that a very important dignitary has arrived! We all know that Carol usually manages to do the impossible, but this is truly incredible—even for her!"

During this speech, Carol and a priest friend ostentatiously rushed out of the room. The drum roll continued and grew to a crescendo. The MC boomed, "Ladies and gentlemen, please rise and greet our distinguished guest!"

Everyone stood; the band started playing "Pomp and Circumstance." All eyes turned to the doorway. There, between Carol and the priest, stood my father, his hand upraised in the familiar papal blessing.

There were gasps of astonishment. For three full minutes, many of the guests actually believed John Paul himself had come to the party. Sure, it was impossible. But, as the MC had stated, Carol often did the impossible. Gradually, however, they began to realize that even she couldn't have pulled this one off. This smiling, waving figure wasn't really the pope.

Of course not. It was someone even more important. At least to me.

I can't help but smile when I picture what has happened now that John Paul II has joined my father in Paradise. I bet they're confusing the hell—I mean—the heck out of God. I am certain they are both looking down from Heaven right now and blessing us all.

Long may they wave.

I'm Right–You're Wrong!

No doubt about it. Whether elections determine winners by the narrowest of questionable margins or by landslides, they don't change the minds of voters. If our candidate wins, great. It's only right, after all. But if he or she loses, the result was a disastrous fluke.

The arguments that support our candidate, our party, our views, are all so logical! So right! So indisputable! Those that bolster the other person's opinion, on the other hand, are ridiculously feeble. We can squabble until Bill Clinton enters a monastery or George Bush learns how to pronounce "nuclear," but nothing we say is going to change the other's mind.

You think the acrimony among various candidates is intense? Hey, that's nothing compared to the bitterness among their supporters, which lingers long after election winners and losers make nice, at least in public.

I don't think it's an exaggeration to say that heated political campaigns and the ensuing results can destroy marriages, demolish friendships, decimate condo communities, and even divide kindergarten classes.

If you love X, you hate Y, and you simply cannot understand how anyone in his or her right mind could possibly disagree. I mean, please! It's so obvious that your choice is the *only* right one. It also follows that you are convinced that Leno, Letterman, and the "Saturday Night Live" cast are undeniably brilliant when they make sarcastic remarks about Y but are slanderous and idiotic when they snipe at X.

I know, I know. I'm wimping out by using alphabetical designations instead of actual IDs; but if I name names, I'll be sure to alienate half my readers. I learned my lesson when I recklessly disclosed my political leanings to my friends Jane and John Doe (no way am I identifying them either). The result was a fiery debate during dinner at their house one night. They are both bullishly X; but Jane, after trying unsuccessfully to shut John up, diplomatically (and cowardly) managed to remove herself from the argument by going out to the kitchen to load the dishwasher, wash the floor, repaint the ceiling, feed the cat. . . . And they don't even have a cat. She borrowed one from next door.

But John didn't need her backup. He was on a roll—eyeballs popping, index finger stabbing, spewing his party's line and grilling me as if I were a suspect in the assassination of Abraham Lincoln. (I swear I had nothing to do with that. I was at home at my spinning wheel at the time.) I kept repeating, "I don't want to discuss it!" But John continued his barrage, even when I blocked my ears and loudly sang "God Bless America." I could have simply gone home, of course, but we hadn't had dessert yet, so leaving really wasn't an option.

A few days later, John phoned. Finally, I thought. An apology. Hardly.

"I don't suppose you've been reading the latest about X and Y," he huffed.

"I most certainly have," I said.

"And what have you learned from that?" he asked triumphantly.

"That I'm right and you're wrong," I retorted. Obviously we had each been reading different sources—I the unbiased, accurate newspapers and magazines and he those that distorted the facts.

Nevertheless, I finally persuaded John and Jane that we should call a truce and banish politics from our conversation. We're grownups, after all. We should be able to rise above endless, childish bickering. To seal the deal, I invited them to my house for dinner next week. It will be a relief to enjoy a relaxing, friendly evening again.

Also, it will give me an opportunity to set them straight on an apparent misconception they have about their religion being better than mine.

Them That Has, Gets

Doesn't it strike you as more than a little unfair that so much largesse seems to fall into the laps of those whose laps are already overflowing?

For example, the gorgeous cheerleader has hunky boyfriends up to her pom-poms, so to speak. The wealthy tycoon is the first to learn about a hot new investment, which doubles his net worth before the echo of the market's opening bell has faded. Frequent flyers get frequent-flyer miles that enable them to fly even more frequently, amassing still more miles as they go. The list goes on and on.

At the top of this inventory of injustice, as far as I'm concerned, are the huge amounts of money made in endorsements by those who already receive outrageous payments for playing games, spitting, scratching their crotches, and screaming obscenities at coaches, umpires, referees, and fans.

Of course, not everyone who reaps these commercial harvests is nasty. Some are perfectly nice people. But so am I. And so are you, I'm sure. Why can't we share this jackpot?

For a million bucks or so, I would have been happy to "just do it" in my Nikes, be photographed with a milk mustache for all the national magazines, or tout the pleasures of a luxury cruise ship, as some celebrities do. Heck, I'd even have agreed to take an expense-paid cruise to authenticate my pitch.

I might have even risked a social call to the Oval Office when Bill Clinton was in residence if *The National Enquirer* made an offer. Alas, they never did.

Even royalty is cashing in. WeightWatchers probably paid one of its first endorsers, Sarah Ferguson, the Duchess of York, enough to buy her own small castle, complete with a well-equipped fitness center. And I doubt that she had to pony up the weekly meeting charge either. In fact, I'm sure she never attended a single one. I, on the other hand, graced them with my presence faithfully—and shelled out my fee every time. But did they offer me a king's (or duchess's) ransom to do commercials for them? Of course not. Apparently rank does have its privileges.

Furthermore, I bet I eat as much Jell-O as Bill Cosby ever did—maybe more—but Kraft Foods never begged my agent for my services to help sell the stuff. Come to think of it, I never had an agent. But that's no excuse. I'll be happy to take the calls of any company directly, or they can e-mail me at OfferLot$aBuck$.com.

And what about William Shatner? His "Star Trek" residuals don't satisfy him? I wonder if I can name my own price to launch him back into outer space and take over his Priceline contract.

The list goes on.

Consider Oprah's former personal chef, Rosie Daley, who I'm sure was rewarded handsomely for her culinary duties and who also then reaped royalties by sharing her recipes in her best-selling book, *In the Kitchen with Rosie.* I have the same first name. Shouldn't that count for something?

As if Regis Philbin wasn't already disgustingly rich, way back when his "Who Wants to Be a Millionaire" quiz show was riding high, he also sponsored a line of "Millionaire" shirts and ties. By contrast, I'd be happy to lend my name to a line of tacky clothes for the financially challenged. Are you listening, Seventh Avenue?

Then there's Liz Taylor, who has mined enough gold from her White Diamonds perfume line to finance the purchase of even more multicolored, high-carat gems to join the others already jammed into her jewelry vault.

And let's not forget George Forman, who is probably making more money touting his grills than he ever did in the ring. Would anyone ever buy one if George wasn't already rich and famous? Seriously. If I were to go on TV peddling my own blend of cellulite cream, for example, would it sell? Of course not. Especially if I had to submit to close-ups. Which gives me an idea. Maybe I can get the Thigh Master people to pay me to assert publicly that I do *not* use their machine. Suzanne Somers can do the "after" shots. I'll be happy to do the "befores"—and at half her salary.

Or, better yet, I could do voiceovers and not have to worry about my appearance at all. I'm sure Lauren Bacall never bothered to slap on lipstick before purring into a microphone to extol the virtues of Fancy Feast to finicky felines.

Yes, I'm envious, but there are a few celebrities who couldn't pay me enough to replace them. For example, June Allyson's old Depends account was always safe from me; I wouldn't have touched it—even with disposable gloves. And Florence Henderson never had to worry about my stealing her Polident commercials. Do you think I'd ever imply on national TV that my teeth and I might not sleep together?

But the award for ultimate bad taste in advertising has to go to Bob Dole and his onetime Viagra pitch. Why in the world would a highly respected former senator go public with his admission that he wasn't up to the job? I know, I know. He did it to help the millions of men who suffer from ED (erectile dysfunction), but I think it was more a case of BD (brain dysfunction).

To prove that I'm not completely bitter about not being in a position to share the endorsements windfall, I'd like to extend kudos to Paul Newman, who uses the proceeds of his Newman's Own products to fund a camp for seriously ill children. He may be losing his looks, but he still has class. I would love to express my feelings in person; so if you're reading this, Paul, let me know where and when we can meet. You can reach me at StillSmitten.com.

We've Got to Stop Meeting Like This

Where did it all begin, this mania for meetings? Back in the Paleolithic Age is my bet. I'm sure anthropologists have come across cave drawings of Fred Flintstone, Barney Rubble, and some of the other guys (no women allowed back then, of course) sitting around a large, flat rock discussing the day's agenda:

1. Read minutes of last meeting.
2. Invent wheel.
3. Discover fire.

Of course, by the time all the attendees finished disputing the accuracy of item No. 1, the sun had gone down; and items 2 and 3 had to be shelved. I'm not sure, but I think they kept getting postponed until the Neolithic Age.

Nothing much has changed. Today, businesspeople the world over spend hour after unproductive hour sitting around talking instead of doing. The setting is different, of course. Ankle-deep plush carpeting instead of dirt floors. Yards of polished-mahogany conference table instead of your basic boulder. Walls decorated with elaborately framed, expensive art instead of hieroglyphics. But the same old yackety-yak, with everyone trying to speak a little louder and a lot longer—it matters not about what—in order to hog the limelight and the boss's attention.

You remember the boss. He's the one who called this meeting in the first place. Why? To develop a new marketing strategy?

To determine why the last quarter was such a disaster? Or even to solicit suggestions for the company picnic? None of the above. The real reason was so *he* could bask in the limelight and enjoy the spectacle of his acolytes trying to out-yes each other.

Let's face it. If Mr. Big wants to confer with his troops, he doesn't have to gather them from the far-flung corners of his empire as did Richard III. Today's fearless leader can simply set up a video conference call, or turn on his computer and chat with his underlings in cyberspace. Instead, the modern CEO often spends mega money to fly the company's executives first class to an exotic tropical island, where he provides lavish suites and gourmet feasts in decadently luxurious hotels. In return they might be expected to attend a poolside meeting and gobble caviar and prime, aged beef while their chief outlines belt-tightening measures to help the company survive the latest tumble of its stock.

Unfortunately, this insanity isn't confined to the private sector. I'd like to have a tax rebate for every time a bunch of Washington VIPs and their staffs fly, first class, to some luxury resort to hold meetings to discuss ways to trim the federal budget. This is standard operating procedure. Our elected and appointed bureaucrats are in perpetual motion, crisscrossing the country and the continents to meet with each other, with officials of other countries, with constituents, or with various special-interest groups. But it's hard to blame them. The example is set at the top. All the recent residents of the Oval Office seem to have spent most of their administrations on gas-guzzling Air Force One, flying to meet with other heads of state. These guys couldn't talk on the phone? I mean, it's not as if they need the frequent-flyer miles to go visit the relatives.

I'd really like to explore this meeting obsession further, but I don't have time right now. I'm already late for my weekly Anti-Meetings Group meeting.

Animal Rights (and Wrongs)

How do people manage today? How do they pay their mortgages and fill the tanks of their SUVs and the tummies and college bank accounts of their kids, while simultaneously financing dance, skiing, skating, gymnastics, swimming, and music lessons? And given all this, how can they support their high-maintenance pets?

It's not like when I was a child. I did have a dog, an adorable little mongrel named Trixie. Pedigree? Papers? Are you kidding? But what she lacked in breeding, she made up for in cuteness and economy. Fortunately, she wasn't a discriminating diner. She happily ate table scraps. Furthermore, Trixie never saw a vet. The word simply wasn't in our family vocabulary, never mind our budget.

Since so much time has passed, I guess it's safe to confess that Trixie was an illegal. She didn't have a license, an extravagance for us back then. Instead, we opted to hope that Trixie would never escape her leash (which was her only "accessory," by the way) and get nabbed by the dogcatcher.

Groomers? Forgeddabout it. Nevertheless, Trixie's silky coat was always shiny. My mom brushed her daily and bathed her weekly in the cellar washtub. And she (Trixie, not Mom) never went to a kennel. We spent family vacations with relatives at the beach, twenty miles from home, and Trixie was always welcome.

Exotic destinations that barred pets weren't a problem. We couldn't afford them anyway.

Today it's different. Now many family pooches and pussycats boast lineages as impressive as those of crown princes, so their treatment must be equally royal. They (the pets, not the princes) dine only on expensive, nutrient-laden kibbles and occasional gourmet treats from "shoppes" specializing in pricey tidbits for the four-legged set. And when their families must leave home without them, they are pampered at exclusive pet hotels. However, many animals aren't always thrilled with such arrangements.

Friends of mine live with Henry, a very independent cat who suffered severe anxiety symptoms whenever he was checked into a classy kennel. Then one time, Henry's usual spacious third-floor accommodations were full, and he was given a pen on the first floor. He loved it. Completely gone was the agitation he had always exhibited once he was "rescued." Now when Henry's roommates travel, they always reserve the lower-level suite for him at his home away from home, and he's one happy cat.

My niece's husky, Timber, was once traumatized by a brief visit to a posh puppy palace, so she now travels with the family whenever possible. When that's not an option, she gets to stay home in the care of a trusted 24/7 sitter who plays with her, feeds her, walks her, and generally ensures her happiness and well-being until her primary caretakers return.

In addition to being doted on, today's pets flaunt fancier wardrobes than some Hollywood luminaries—gem-encrusted collars; brightly colored coats; and rainy-day slickers, boots, and harnesses with attached umbrellas. (I swear! I saw one yesterday.)

And let's not forget medical care. Today's bills for rabies shots, distemper, worms, ear infections, and dozens of other mammal maladies can make an eminent pediatrician's fees seem paltry.

But that's not all. There's also pet psychiatry. I'm serious. Last Tuesday a woman in the grocery-store checkout line asked to go ahead of me. She was late for an appointment with her cat Peek-a-Boo's psychiatrist ($200 for three sessions). Apparently the fourteen-year-old feline had recently started urinating on the expensive upholstery, beds, and Persian rugs. Could it be because the cat is old and incontinent? No, no! According to Peek's shrink, she has developed issues with the family and is expressing her anger. (Maybe because they make her wear a red umbrella with her chartreuse boots?)

Another friend recently bought a hermit crab for her daughter. It's been two weeks now, and the crab still hasn't come out of its shell. Sounds like a classic case of Social Anxiety Disorder.

I gave my friend the phone number of Peek-a-Boo's analyst.

Born Too Soon

My nightmare has come true. I've become one of those old fogies who say things like, "Kids today! They don't know how lucky they are!"

I'm jealous. I admit it. I envy the opportunities they take for granted, the advantages I never had: breakfast with Mickey and friends at Disneyland at age six, a car at sixteen, a year of study abroad at nineteen. And later, at least three weeks paid vacation, profit sharing, dental insurance—and a shot at VIPdom for every Jack *and* Jill.

Not so in the Dark Ages, when I was young. Back then, career choices were limited for girls. (That's right, girls. Not even our grandmothers were called women then.) Except for the rare female who was aggressive enough to ignore the rules, most of us docilely trained to become teachers, nurses, or secretaries. I now find it incredible that we meekly accepted these boundaries, but at the time I didn't question it.

I was so thoroughly brainwashed that, though I had always loved writing, it never occurred to me as a vocational possibility. That was man's work. I knew my place—at the blackboard, in front of the class; by the bedside, bedpan in hand; or in the boardroom, taking notes.

First I considered teaching. I thought about the satisfaction of molding young minds. I thought about summers off and not having to go to work when it snowed. I thought about dealing daily with bratty kids and irate parents. I thought I didn't want to teach, after all.

Nursing I didn't even think about. I have a germ phobia. I get paranoid at the movies if somebody sneezes—onscreen.

So I chose the only field that was left and enrolled in Boston University's bachelor of commercial science program, a euphemism for chauvinistic serfdom (note the identical initials). I was convinced that my mission in life was to help some man rise through the corporate ranks and become president of his company. My reward? A puny (but private!) cubicle outside the Great One's spacious, windowed suite, and a china pot in which to brew his tea, rather than the aluminum ones used by the secretaries of lesser personages. To achieve this wondrous goal, I spent four years studying shorthand, typing, and unquestioning respect for my boss of the future.

N.B., "boss," singular. When we agreed to work for someone in those days, it was presumed to be until death or mandatory retirement did us part. The only other acceptable reason for a woman to leave a job was matrimony. In fact, not only was she permitted to leave without stigma when she got married, she was expected to. Everyone knew that a woman who hadn't managed to snag a husband in school worked only to meet an eligible man (again, singular) and get married. Once she reached this pinnacle, she was supposed to retire to the kitchen and bedroom. If for some reason she retained her job after marriage and became pregnant (is it all right to use that word for a mixed audience now?), she was expected to resign immediately, preferably as soon as the rabbit died (yes, a bunny had to be sacrificed to determine pregnancy back then), or at least before its funeral. Why? Because no respectable woman wanted to be seen in public in "that condition." Everyone would know how she got that way.

Those of us who weren't successful (i.e., weren't wearing an engagement ring with our caps and gowns) set about meekly to serve our life sentences in the first company that did us the honor of hiring us after graduation. Again, the brainwashing was very effective. I stayed in my first job for fourteen years. During that time, I never questioned being overworked, underpaid, and generally taken for granted. When my boss's department's bottom line was bottoming out, he frantically hired more salesmen to generate more revenue, but never an extra secretary. The budget, you know. "Rose will do your typing" was part of his welcoming speech to each of those eager dynamos who were anxious to make themselves visible. They did this by writing volumes of memos, letters, and reports—which, of course, I typed. I also did their filing, tracked their appointments, answered their phones, made their travel reservations, and constructed their expense reports from whatever bits and pieces of information I could salvage from their attaché cases (my first professional creative writing experience). I did this days, nights, weekends, and even on several holidays. And I did it without one word of complaint or one penny of overtime pay. It was never offered, and I never asked. Discuss money? Not me. I was a *nice* girl.

But I was happy in my little world. Hey, I was one of the privileged. I worked for a department head! Eventually I was rewarded with a promotion as secretary to my boss's boss, a division manager. And the Idiot of the Century. I do not bestow such titles lightly. The man earned it. He never dictated (couldn't think fast enough) but instead scrawled his letters in longhand and insisted I type them exactly as written. He felt threatened if I changed one misspelled word, misplaced punctuation mark, or ungrammatical phrase. He knew I liked to write, you see, and he wanted to establish immediately that he could write better.

I tried not to tamper with his prose. I really did. But I soon stopped putting my initials on his letters lest anyone think I was the stupid one. Either he didn't notice, or he approved. After all, my initials weren't on his originals.

One day he handed me a letter he had written to a nanny in England whom he was considering importing to look after his children. "For the sake of convenience," his scrawl said, "I am sending you this letter instead of my wife." Granted, it would have been much less convenient to stuff her into the envelope, but I knew he didn't mean that. Though he didn't deserve it, I thought I'd do him a favor and try to slip one by him. I typed, "For the sake of convenience, I am writing this letter instead of my wife." I still wasn't crazy about it, but I wanted to change it as little as possible, hoping he wouldn't notice. Silly me. He had memorized every golden word.

He dove into my wastebasket and retrieved his longhand version. "*This* is what I wrote," he said, his index finger stabbing the sentence, "and this is what I want you to type!" Instead, I typed my letter of resignation and hit the road. Unfortunately, it turned out to be a dead end lined with more secretarial pit stops. But eventually, hallelujah! I managed to tunnel through and land a job as operations manager of a theater chain. I became a friend to the stars. I negotiated contracts with Actors Equity. Directors (who had no idea that my only prior stage experience was when I played *Amapola* at a piano recital when I was nine) asked my advice about blocking.

Who says there is no God? I just wish She had led me to glory two decades earlier, or arranged for me to be born two decades later. Because young women today, they don't know how lucky they are.

www.technophobia.com or Can You Drown While Surfing the Net?

Here we are—riding the wave of the golden age of technology! Isn't it exciting? Well, not to everyone. In fact, many golden agers refuse to acknowledge the entire phenomenon, hoping it will go away.

I know, because many of my contemporaries suffer from terminal technophobia. As far as they are concerned, Thomas Edison is responsible for most of the world's ills. Electricity is a foolish extravagance, which they would prefer to do without if at all possible. In fact, one of my friends does. Sharon lives in an unwired, remote area of Maine and makes do with a generator, which she uses only for an hour or two a day when absolutely necessary.

And if my friends consider Thomas Edison a villain, that gives you a clue as to how they feel about Henry Ford. Despite that, however, out of sheer necessity, they all do have a car in the driveway instead of a horse and buggy in the barn. They would prefer the latter, but the old gray mare is not a feasible choice in today's environment. Parking a horse at the mall or the local supermarket (both of which they abhor, of course) would be a problem. No hitching posts.

In our youth, before any of us could afford automobiles or other newfangled gadgets, my friends considered me to be quite respectable and sensible. Not anymore. Marie and Nancy started

having their doubts years ago when I acquired a touchtone telephone. It was bad enough that our grandparents were forced to
say farewell to the friendly operator who placed their calls and
to accept rotary dialing instead. And now push buttons.
Ridiculous frivolity. Marie stubbornly refuses to relinquish her
old rotary phone despite her increasing frustrations with reach-
ing voicemail systems that require touchtone to make menu
selections. You don't even want to get her started on that subject. Trust me.

Furthermore, since she lives in a three-story house with her
single rotary museum piece, she cannot understand why I need
three phones in a one-level, five-room condo. As for memory
dialing, redialing, call forwarding, and call waiting? Foolish
excess!

Then there's my voicemail. Ridiculous. So what if I miss a
call or two? my friends reason. Who's going to be calling me
who's so important he or she can't call back? And, of course,
they feel that my cell phone is pretentious beyond belief. They
don't buy my explanation that I have it only for emergency use.
It's true. I have an inexpensive prepaid service that provides
only a very limited number of minutes; so if I need to make a
non-urgent call while on the road, I'll go miles out of my way to
find a pay phone first. But my friends are convinced that I spend
hours tootling down the highway with my flip phone to my ear,
chatting aimlessly with no one in particular, just to look cool.
And at my age. How pitiful. Obviously the death rays from my
absurd microwave oven have fried my brain.

And why in God's name do I possibly need two television sets
and two VCRs? One TV they would forgive, since they each
caved in years ago and acquired one. Janet even has cable. And,
amazingly, Irene and Nancy also each own a VCR. Irene
received hers as a gift two years ago and has never plugged it in.
Nancy bought hers to tape her favorite PBS show in case it is

scheduled to air at a time she can't be home. However, she adamantly refuses to learn to program it. Instead, if the show begins in six hours, and she plans to be out all day and not home in time, she puts a long-playing tape into the VCR and starts the recording before she leaves. The fact that I actually learned to program both my VCRs is further evidence that I must be in league with the devil.

The ultimate proof of this sacrilegious affiliation was the purchase of my first computer decades ago. Good Lord, why? I obviously had gone completely berserk. And they have no idea how much I paid for it back then. If they ever find out, they'll cart me off to the nearest loony bin and offer novenas day and night to whatever saint is in charge of the hopelessly demented and corrupt.

They probably think I'm using my computer to seduce teenage boys on a chat line. They've heard about degenerates who surf the net. They're not sure what "surfing the net" means, but they know it's evil. What other reason could I possibly have for buying such a device? Yes, they know I write, but what was wrong with my old IBM Selectric? Heaven knows, it took them years to accept even that. "Progress" may have forced our forebears to abandon quill pens in favor of typewriters, but why the need to switch from the Royal manuals we all learned on? They worked perfectly well.

I try to explain all the wondrous worlds the Internet can access—all the books in the Library of Congress, the New York Public Library's reference desk, entire encyclopedias complete with audio and video, worldwide news, up-to-the-minute stock-market information, medical updates, genealogical data, consumer protection reports, the complete works of Shakespeare, movie reviews, a wealth of immediately accessible travel information, the ability to make instant reservations . . . and so much more. Like a proud parent, I tell them that my computer is so smart it actually changes its own clock from standard to daylight savings time and vice versa. I gush about the convenience of e-mail, the marvelous graphics, online foreign-language courses, cooking demos, home maintenance tips . . . I offer to demonstrate some of these wonders. Forget it. They refuse to get within twenty feet of what they consider the infernal contraption, even if it's turned off. Do they fear they will be contaminated just by osmosis? Maybe if I give them crosses to hold and garlic bulbs to hang around their necks, they might risk getting closer. Then, again, maybe not.

They're happy in their non-tech cocoons, and I'm too busy shopping for my next-generation digital camera to keep trying to coax them out. I wonder how this will all be resolved in Paradise. Do you suppose we'll be given a choice of accommodations in the Garden of Bygone Days or the Eden of Electronic Wonders? I know which they'd choose, of course. And me? Well, they've been my friends forever, after all; and we always swore nothing would come between us.

I'll really miss them.

You Can't Beat This Deal!

I'd rather have root canal than shop for a new car. Seriously. With root canal, you have Novocain to blunt the pain, and you don't have to play that ridiculous game of price negotiation. It would be pretty weird if you did.

Picture this: Soft music surrounds you as you repose on a buttery-soft leather recliner. (Remember when you used to sit upright at the dentist's on cold, unyielding Naugahyde?) Enter the endodontist. He extends his hand.

"Hi! I'm Joe Jones. Here's my card. Glad to see you. It's a pleasure to meet a woman with good taste and intelligence."

"Huh?"

"Hey! You chose us over the competition. Smart lady!"

"Huh?"

"Ha, ha! And a sense of humor, too! That's great. I'm really going to enjoy doing business with you. . . . Now, which one of our procedures are you interested in? Let me guess. I'll bet someone as discriminating as you has her heart set on our new top-of-the-line, four-canal job that we advertised in Sunday's *Tribune Gazette*—right?"

"Well, I'd love it, naturally. But there's no way I can afford it. I don't have dental insurance. . . . "

"Bummer! Well, how much are you planning to spend?"

"As little as possible; I'm on a pretty tight budget."

"Tell me about it. Tough times. But you're really in luck! Just this morning, we slashed the price on our popular two-canal procedure. Between you and me, the four-canal job is really overkill. Sure, it has a certain snob appeal, but that's not you. You're above that sort of thing. I can tell."

"Well, I don't know. Are X-rays and Novocain standard with the two-canal?"

"I knew you had a sense of humor! I like you, so I'm going to bend the rules and throw in the X-rays, but the Novocain is an option."

"How much?"

"One hundred twenty-five dollars."

"One twenty-five?! That much?"

"Okay, okay! I'm a sucker for a good negotiator. My associate's not in today—when he finds out, he'll kill me—but I'm going to let you have the Novocain for $119.95. We're losing money at that price, but it's yours. Now, open wide!"

And suppose the same practices applied to clothing purchases.

Scene two: You're in your favorite department store looking for a new dress. You see one you like. The sticker price is $349. You gasp. A salesperson materializes before you can escape to the clearance rack.

"I can see you're surprised by that price," she says. "I don't blame you. I swear they made a mistake when they were ticketing; but that's what it says, so that's all I'll charge you. It's gorgeous! An original copy of an Origami knockoff. It would be a steal at $500! But I'm sure you know that. Will that be cash or charge?"

"Neither. It's way out of my price range, I'm afraid."

"I just remembered! I got a memo this morning about a sale the store is planning next week. If you can wait a minute while I check with my boss, I may be able to persuade her to let me mark this one down for you today!"

She returns in ten minutes. She's beaming.

"What sign are you? Obviously the stars are on your side today! She said yes! That means I can take 15 percent off this already unbelievably low price! Will that be cash or charge?"

"I'm afraid I still can't justify it. I mean, the party I need it for isn't really that important. . . . "

"Every party is important! A lot of people will be there. Their first impression of you will be based on your appearance. You can't afford *not* to look your best! Look, I really want you to have this dress. Let me see if I can talk my boss out of another 5 percent. I can't promise, but . . . "

"No, really. It's lovely, but it's just beyond my budget."

She cools perceptibly. "I see. Well, let me show you something from our previously owned, low-mileage collection. . . . "

Same premise, different locale. Scene three: The supermarket checkout line. Action!

Checkout clerk, weighing grapes: "You certainly have an eye for quality! A perfect bunch! Those will be $1.98."

"I don't know. I don't think they're really fresh. See those two brown ones there?"

"They probably just got bruised when you stuffed them into the plastic bag. But I'll deduct thirteen cents, if you promise not to tell my supervisor. . . . "

"Well, okay. Now, about this cantaloupe. I'm not sure I want it. I mean, it looks good, but the price is way out of line."

"You know, of course, that cantaloupes are loaded with carotene and that carotene is an effective cancer preventive. Can you put a price on your family's health? Just five minutes ago, I checked your neighbor, Mrs. Jones, through. She bought two cantaloupes at the same price as these. Do the Joneses deserve better health than your family?"

"Okay, okay. But this dog food is a different story. Don't you have something less expensive?"

"The Joneses feed their dog that very same Frisky Peps."

"The Joneses' Fang is four months old. Our Fido has fourteen years on his odometer, and he has no teeth. He couldn't even chew Frisky Peps. All he needs is some economy-grade mush to get his motor started in the morning. . . . "

And you have twenty-three more items to go. What a nightmare. Imagine how much time you'd have to spend at the grocery store, to say nothing of prior research—comparative shopping in at least four other supermarkets, plus trips to the library to check out *Consumer Reports'* weekly *Veggie Values,* the *Blue Book of Beef Bargains,* and the *Wall Street Journal's* latest bottle trade-in quotations.

Just thinking about it exhausts me. I have to get my mind off it. I think I'll go to a movie. But seven dollars! That's outrageous! I'll offer five bucks, tops. Not a penny more. Unless they throw in a large popcorn.

You Should Have Been Here Last Week! (Or How I Found Out the Red Sox Won the Pennant)

Do you ever get the feeling that your whole life is running at least a week late? Mine is. Maybe it's because I was overdue at birth, so I've been behind ever since. If I could ever catch up, I'd have it made. Because, my friends, the secret to success and happiness is not beauty, brains, or talent. It's timing. And, boy, is mine ever off.

As a teenager, I'd go to Cape Cod with my girlfriends. Dullsville! All the other girls there said, "Gee, you should have been here last weekend. It was wall-to-wall boys!"

Later I'd take a trip to New Hampshire for the foliage. Only there wasn't any. Oh, there were leaves all right, but they had all turned brown. "If only you had come last week," I'd be told. "The colors were spectacular!"

In the winter, I'd trek back to New Hampshire to ski, and I'd arrive just as an unseasonable heat wave was melting all the snow that had been fantastic the week before. So I'd head south to Florida to cavort in the surf, but I couldn't because the jellyfish were having a convention. Last week, needless to say, the water was gorgeous—and fishless.

Come spring, I'd go to Washington, D.C., bringing with me a cold snap that killed the last of the cherry blossoms just as my plane touched down.

In fact, wherever or whenever I go, the first thing I usually hear from the hotel desk clerk are the chilling words, "The season is over." Do you know what that means? It means that if you haven't brought your knitting along to while away the quiet hours, you've got big trouble. On one such memorable trip, I did manage to find a small shop that was open, by some fluke. The owner probably needed a rest and decided that was the best place to get it at that time of year. Out of sheer boredom I started spending with wild abandon. Heck, what's a vacation for? I then asked if I might have a shopping bag for my parcels. The shopkeeper shook his head and said, "I'm sorry, I don't have any. The season is over." Bummer. When you can't even make the shopping-bag season, you *know* you're a loser.

Way back in another century (well, 1963 to be exact), my friend Irma and I went to Zermatt, Switzerland, and managed to hit it during the one-week slump between the end of the summer season and the beginning of the winter season. Since there was no one else to talk to, our big entertainment was to go yell at the Matterhorn so we could hear it yell back. Understandably, a little of this mad excitement goes a long way; so after a couple of days of such stimulating activity, I decided it would be much more fun to do some laundry. As it turned out, it was.

While I was in the bathroom rinsing out a few things, I heard voices. Human voices. Not an Alpine echo, but an actual conversation. They were coming from the suite next door, loud and clear, apparently amplified by the plumbing and tile. I was fascinated. My neighbors (a socialite couple from Boston, I gathered from their discussion) were having a humdinger of an argument about everything from her money (which she accused him of spending on himself rather than investing for her) to his business affairs (which, not having been born yesterday, she knew were not strictly business). Then they got around to fighting over their Swiss sojourn. It seems that when she wanted to go home, he absolutely couldn't leave because of pressing business there. But now, just because the Red Sox had won the pennant, suddenly they had to rush home so he wouldn't miss the World Series. So the Red Sox had pulled it off! This was news to me. We hadn't seen a newspaper in days.

I burst into the bedroom, where Irma was knitting (she's smarter and more realistic than I, you see—she had brought hers along). "Guess what!" I exclaimed. "The Red Sox won the pennant!" She dropped three stitches, and to this day she hasn't figured out how I learned that in a radioless bathroom in the shadow of the Matterhorn.

To further illustrate how bad my travel timing is, I once got to Capistrano a week after the swallows arrived. The travel agent had convinced me they were going to be late that year. A little bird told him.

I am finally resigned to the fact that, wherever I go, at least three or more of the following are bound to be true:

- The midnight sun shone brighter last week.
- The eligible millionaires were all here last week.
- The sunsets were more spectacular last week.
- It wasn't as crowded last week.
- There were lots of interesting people here last week.
- Armani had an incredible sale last week.
- The wine festival ended last week.
- The grass was greener last week.

But I don't have to travel to be in the wrong time zone. I manage very well right here at home. For example, the other night a friend took me to a trendy club where it turned out that, for that evening only, they were featuring local amateur "talent." Not only was the show unbelievably bad, but the place was a mess—wrecked by all the enthusiastic fans who had been there last week for a super star-studded spectacular.

Remember that old dance, the Funky Chicken? Well, I finally learned to do it a week after it died and went to the great barnyard in the sky. I also personally insured the demise of the Electric Slide and the Macarena.

Furthermore, the week after I had my hair cropped to one-inch fuzzy ringlets, long and sleek became the only acceptable style. And do you know how long it takes my hair to grow? Just long enough so that short and curly will be back "in."

But I do have my good days now and then. Take last Thursday. That was a beauty! When I checked the winning lottery number in the paper, I saw it was mine! I was ecstatic—until I noticed that I was reading last week's paper, and, of course, I hadn't bought a ticket then.

Well, I've cried on your shoulder long enough. I'd better wrap this up and send it to my editor. Excuse me a second while I check my calendar for the submission deadline. . . .

Dammit! It was last week!

Like, Whatever . . . Ya Know

I'd like to voice a few pet peeves wordwise. However, first I must ask: Can one "voice" an opinion in writing? How can a peeve be a pet? Are "wise" words, such as "wordwise," correct grammarwise?

But back to my peeves.

High on my list are misplaced "only"s, such as "this insurance policy only covers passengers on nonregulated airlines." How fortunate. If it *un*covered them, they might catch cold.

Another vexation is superfluous apostrophes in plurals, like *The Smith's,* often seen on front doors or mailboxes. And how about "the dog wagged it's tail" (which I read in a children's story recently)? Hey, I like a happy dog as much as the next person, but "it's"? Also, years ago, a shop in my city called itself Audreys' Hideaway. It is possible, of course, that the establishment was owned by more than one woman named Audrey, but I doubt it. How many Audreys do you know of since the lovely Ms. Hepburn is no more? A local store solves the apostrophe problem by displaying *Jokers Wild* on one sign and *Joker's Wild* on another. It's impossible to tell if they're talking about multiple unruly pranksters or simply stating that one jester is untamed.

And what's with conversations like the following between two young ladies (at least I think they were females—sometimes hard to tell these days) that I overheard on the bus yesterday:

"So he goes, 'Yeah, well, ya know, why should I?' And I go,

'Well, like, ya know . . . whatever.' And he goes . . . "

Exactly where is everybody going? It's like, ya know, sooo irritating.

Another problem is gender political correctness, which has introduced a whole new area of grammatical inconsistency. Why do advertisers persist in saying things like: *If your child is having reading problems, this program will help them.* Why not change *child is* to *children are*, so the rest of the sentence will be correct? And a recent Walt Disney promo proclaims: *A child lives in a world of their own imagination.* It would not have been so hard to say, *Children live in a world of their own imagination.* If you pay attention, you'll hear and read countless similar references, all written by copywriters who are getting paid big bucks.

Though all the above really bug me (how did insects get into this?), the phrase that irritates me the most is "more importantly," instead of simply "more important." One hears this from educators, corporation presidents, the clergy, radio and television personalities, and others who should know better but still say things such as "more importantly, February usually has twenty-eight days." Actually, they don't often talk about February, but you know what I mean. Would these people proclaim Tom Cruise to be "more handsomely" than Brad Pitt? Or would they judge Martha Stewart's duck à l'orange to be "more deliciously" than that prepared by Emeril Lagasse? Since I have never met Tom or Brad personally nor have I been invited to dine with Martha or Emeril, I'm in no position to make comparisons. However, if I were, I'd at least do it in a grammatically correct (certainly not "correctly") fashion.

Of course, I'm not an authority. I could be wrong about any or all of this. After all, I've been wrong before—once in 1943, and again in 1952, as I recall.

This compulsion to correct everything I hear and read, from radio and television commercials to billboards on the highway, is a curse. I don't have a moment's respite. I beg you, please help me before I edit again!

If You Can't Stand the Heat . . .

My mother was a terrific cook. I am not. I never bothered to learn because I figured that when the time came that I had to rely on my own cooking, all I'd need would be recipes. Anyone who can read, I reasoned, can cook—which is true, up to a point. But how well? Ah, there's the rub.

Living alone, I have not had in-house critics to provide feedback for my culinary efforts, and friends whom I invite to dinner are not going to gag and say, "Ugh! This is awful!" even if it is. That's why they're friends.

It was with some trepidation, therefore, that I entered the kitchen of my hostess, the legendary actress Joan Fontaine, one long-ago Thanksgiving morning, to offer my assistance. Acting is not Miss Fontaine's only talent. Not by a long shot. She is also a hole-in-one golfer, a prizewinning fisherwoman, a hot-air balloonist, an accomplished horsewoman, and a pilot. "When you've had as many husbands as I've had, darling," she quips, "you learn all their hobbies." And one hobby all hubbies shared was enjoying good food. No problem. Joan is also a gourmet cook who studied at the Cordon Bleu in Paris.

No wonder I was intimidated that day. But though my mother did not teach me to cook, she did teach me good manners, so I asked, politely, "What can I do to help, Joan?" "Can you cook?" she asked. "Not really," I said truthfully, "but I should be able to manage some simple tasks." "All right," said she. "You can section the fruit for the salad."

She handed me an apron and sat me down at a table in front of a large bowl, a bag full of oranges and grapefruit, and a paring knife. I figured, how hard can this be? I found out. She stopped me as I was mangling orange No. 1. "No, no—not that way—this way," she said, demonstrating. Within seconds, she had removed the skin expertly, in one long piece, and then cut into the orange. With one swoop, she sliced into a segment and up the other side, removing a perfect orange slice and leaving behind only the membrane from both sides. In less than a minute, she had repeated this feat until all that was left in her hand was a complete "empty" orange—only membranes and core.

I tried to imitate her. Disaster. "Never mind," she said, "I'll do it. It will be faster." "See, that's why I can't cook," I wailed. "That's what my mother always says." "Good God, I don't blame her," said Joan. "The woman should be canonized just for letting you near her kitchen!" She then banished me to the den to write place cards.

I have never lived it down. Thirty years later in a phone conversation, after her usual, "How's your love life, darling?" (which she knows never compared to hers, even in my wildest dreams), she twisted the knife: "Are you having any more success in your kitchen than in your bedroom these days?" This, in spite of the fact that a mutual friend who had dined at my home a few years ago wrote her a glowing review of the meal. Instead of a letter, he inserted the message in a large mockup of a front page of the show-biz bible, *Variety*. Echoing *GARBO TALKS*, the historic headline touting Greta Garbo's first talking picture, his headline read, *MULA COOKS!*

Unfortunately, his praise gave me a false sense of security. Shortly thereafter, I created a culinary catastrophe. I'd had a busy day. I was ravenous but too tired to cook something from scratch. I decided to make a little pasta topped with some left-over tomato sauce I had in the fridge. I boiled some linguini, warmed the sauce in the microwave, and poured it on the pasta. Strange. It looked quite pink. But I thought that could have been because the lighting in my kitchen isn't very bright. Also, I fig-ured that the thin, flat linguini didn't hold the sauce as well as the lined rigatoni I usually use. So I piled on some grated Romano and dug in. It tasted sweet. Hmmm. I never use sugar in my sauce. But I really was starved, so I kept wolfing it down. As I got to the bottom of the dish, I remembered that I had put onions and a little red pepper in the sauce. This definitely had neither. Then I thought that possibly I had inadvertently used plain crushed tomatoes, since when I don't use a whole can, I save the remainder in a bowl. But as I kept eating, I finally real-ized that it didn't taste the least bit like tomatoes. Then it hit me. A couple of nights before, I was looking for a container to take to my watercolor class. I remembered pouring something out of a half-filled jar in my refrigerator into a bowl so I could use the jar. What I had poured into the bowl was cranberry-apple sauce. Can you imagine that on pasta? With grated Romano yet? Some say it was probably better than my homemade tomato sauce.

Unfortunately, I think they're right.

0! The $ky I$ Falling!

My parents—and my financial adviser—warned me there'd be days like this. But back in the heady late 1990s, who believed them? Not me. Even my very conservative mutual fund annuities were soaring, showing gains of 30 percent, 40 percent, and more. It seemed that my security was assured. I was going to be a rich old lady. I'd travel the globe in style, and when I took my final journey, I'd leave behind some wealthy, happy heirs. Well, not too happy, since their joy at their financial gain would, hopefully, be tempered by their tragic loss. "Why did she have to go?" they'd wail, as they cashed their tear-stained inheritance checks. At least that's how I pictured it.

That scenario changed at the turn of the twenty-first century. I no longer saw myself flying first class to Paris on a whim for a weekend at the Georges Cinq, followed by a deluxe excursion to Venice on the Orient Express. Even the commuter rail to nearby Boston for pizza in the North End began to look like an extravagance.

My aforementioned financial guru tried to reassure me. "You're not going to outlive your money, Rose," he promised.

"Oh, God!" I replied. "Does that mean I'm going to die next week?"

He assured me that the market would bounce back stronger than ever. I'm still waiting.

The one bright spot in this dismal financial climate is Al-Qaeda. Why? Because they have effectively cured my travel bug. I no longer have the slightest desire to fly to Paris, or anywhere at all. I'm even curtailing my excursions to large shopping malls, sports arenas, and theaters (all of which are excellent terrorist targets, as the media helpfully keeps pointing out to them). Friends are still traveling to exotic worldwide destinations. Am I jealous? Not anymore. I'm having enough trouble dealing with the anthrax threat in my own mailbox, thank you, without also worrying about suicidal hijackers in the sky and fanatic bombers at popular tourist attractions.

I know I should follow my president's and the Office of Homeland Security's instructions to carry on as usual, even if a Code Red alert is issued. I should continue to frequent the malls and spend with wild abandon, to dine out often, to support our troubled airlines and hotels by traveling extensively . . . And I would do all that, of course, if I could. I'm as patriotic as the next person. But I really have to tighten my belt right now, so I'm forced to stay home.

Hey, it's as good an excuse as any.

A Curlyhead's Complaint

I had bad hair days long before the phrase was coined. I was an adorable toddler (if it's true that cameras don't lie), but my adorableness (okay, so I can coin words, too) was a fact *despite* rampant ringlets that stuck out crazily all over my head, dipping over mid-forehead and receding at the temples—the hairline of a middle-aged man, which I have to this day.

Yes, I did say ringlets, and yes, I do have naturally curly hair. "You're so lucky!" say my friends whose sleek tresses I would trade my Jaguar for—that is, if I had a Jaguar. They assume that since my hair has a natural curl, it will fall into any style I wish. *Wrong!* If it did, would I look like this? On purpose?

As others who are similarly cursed know well, naturally curly hair does its own thing. You can wind it around huge rollers for hours, soak it in anti-frizz solution, and spray it with enough industrial-strength glop to coax it into different configurations; and it may work—for three minutes and forty-two seconds tops. After that, it goes *boing!* and springs right back to its original, unruly state. And if there is just a trace of humidity in the air, you can even forget about the three minutes and forty-two seconds.

Unfortunately, it has taken me almost my entire life to acknowledge that. God knows why. Obviously, I was in denial. I battled my tenacious tendrils for years and spent enough on hair-smoothing products to support all the wives and children of a colony of bigamists before I finally "got" it and stopped trying to reverse nature.

I'm not any happier about the way I look, but at last I've learned to accept it and go with it, to a point. I definitely have stopped trying to straighten my hair, but I still haven't completely given up my attempts to shape it to my liking. I do this by mercilessly snipping off any wayward coil that spoils the symmetry I am trying to achieve. The results, as you can imagine, are often quite interesting and have been known to launch many hairdressers into fits of hysteria when I flee to them for repairs.

I recall, in particular, a stylist on the Champs Elysées. I was vacationing in beautiful, sophisticated Paris, where I felt definitely un-chic. I decided to splurge and treat myself to a Parisian "do." When Monsieur François sat me down to assess what he had to work with, he paled. For a moment, I was afraid he was going to faint. "Who did this to you?!" he demanded, his eyes misting, his voice trembling. Do you think I was going to admit the disaster was self-inflicted? Not on your life. "A hairdresser back home," I lied. His next comments, though in French that was beyond my rudimentary grasp, left no doubt that he was condemning all American hairdressers to a special hell. Poor François had met his match. Two hours and several hundred francs later, I didn't look much better. I left Paris.

Unfortunately, my next trip was to a tropical paradise—Maui to most people; Frizz City to me. How I envied the lovely Hawaiian girls their satiny long locks that undulated in the sultry breezes as gracefully as did their grass skirts.

Today, of course, curls are in. Some women (and a few men) actually have corkscrew permanents. Go figure. Too bad I wasn't born into this era. Just thinking about the time, money, and aggravation I could have saved myself—and still been fashionable—is enough to make my hair stand straight on end.

Yeah, right. Wishful thinking.

Computer Hell

Remember how computers were supposed to change our lives? They would eliminate paper—no more file cabinets. (Ha!) They would save us time. Less drudgery, more leisure. (Double ha!) They would make us more productive. We would demolish mountains of work in minutes. (Hysterical laughter.)

Since owning a computer, I am ashamed to admit I have used so much paper that I probably am personally responsible for the decimation of an entire forest somewhere in the world. After my first system crash, I became compulsive about printing out everything. Yes, I back up my files, but who can guarantee that nothing will happen to my backups?

However, though I've become an environmentalist's worst nightmare, I am the economists' darling. I can take credit for contributing to the increase in sales of office furniture, because I have to keep buying file cabinets to store all my printouts. Soon I'll also boost real-estate sales, because I'll have to move to a larger house. No room here for any more filing cabinets.

And the manufacturers of printer cartridges have me to thank for their booming profits. I go through cartridges like a kid through a new box of crayons. (The crayons are considerably cheaper.)

And where are all those hours I was supposed to save?

What is so time-consuming are not the things I do on my

computer but the things I try to do that don't work. After fruit-less minutes (okay, okay—days) of trial and error, I call tech support, where, after pressing numerous menu choices, I am, of course, put on hold, the limbo of the damned. I have been sub-jected to more canned music in the last few years than the majority of sane people (i.e., those who do not own computers) hear in a lifetime. And when my call that is so important to them finally connects me to a live techie, my troubles are not over. Oh no, my friend, in many cases they have just begun. Consider the following actual conversation I had early this morning (at three o'clock) with tech support:

Me: I'm having a problem downloading pictures.

TS: I don't know about that. I never downloaded nothing [*sic*].

Me: Well, can you transfer me to someone who does know?

TS: No. Everyone else is busy.

For this I waited on hold for twenty-three minutes.

The time wasn't completely wasted, though. I played comput-er Free Cell solitaire while waiting . . . and after I hung up . . . for another hour and a half. I'm hopelessly addicted.

I take back what I said about the stuff that works not neces-sarily being time-consuming. One application works too well. E-mail. You can't kill it. It just keeps proliferating. I am now on the address list of every computer owner I've known since I was two years old. I've decided it's possible to have too many friends, despite what Mother always told me. These friends send me messages. I thank them. They thank me for thanking them. . . . It's an unending loop. As for the jokes that keep making the rounds, enough already! I just don't have the time for all this entertainment. I really should be attending to some serious stuff—like trying to figure out how to stamp out spam, especial-ly porn. I never search the net for anything even slightly risqué (I swear), but somehow my e-mail address has found its way to the purveyors of messages with subject lines such as "Pictures of Hot Nude Teenage Girls." As if at my age I need to be reminded how grotesque I look by comparison. The breast enlargement pitches I can at least understand, but why oh why do I keep getting e-mails touting formulas guaranteed to enlarge my penis?

But my problems are insignificant compared to those of my friend Joan, who just bought a new computer—one with more bells and whistles than a calliope. She wanted to be sure she had all the latest enhancements that would enrich her life (cue hysterical laughter again). Her computer has ten times the features of mine—and a hundred times the headaches, since problems increase exponentially with each additional application.

I can truthfully say that my computer has changed my life. I now have no life. No time for one. Gotta keep on top of that e-mail and all the other stuff on the Web. I got up at 6:30 this morning. It's now 2:00 P.M., and I'm still sitting at the keyboard—sleep deprived, not dressed, not showered, bed unmade, newspaper unread, and unreachable by phone since I can't afford a separate line for this electronic monster that has me in its grip.

They'll find me some day, slumped over my keyboard, babbling incoherently, desperately trying to boot up one last time.

JohnPaul2@vatican.com

I read a few years ago that the ancient shrine of Our Lady of Guadalupe in Mexico had entered the computer age by launching its own Web site. Even more surprising was the fact that the first visitor to sign onto the site, using a laptop computer, was none other than Pope John Paul II.

The pope at the computer. It's an anachronism—hard to imagine. Sort of like running into Michelangelo at the local pizzeria: "A large cheese with pepperoni, please, but light on the sauce. It makes such a mess when it drips onto my palette."

Can you picture it? John Paul, in his robes and fancy hat, sitting on the papal throne, hammering out an e-mail on his laptop, playing a little computer solitaire, surfing the net, ordering a new Bible at Amazon.com, maybe visiting a chat room . . . How do you suppose he described himself? "Single, flashy dresser with a unique automobile, charismatic, popular, somewhat of a celebrity, world traveler, multilingual, palatial home with large staff, many interests—in younger days enjoyed skiing, acting, and playwriting . . . "

Did he swear when his computer crashed? Did he get fast connections to tech support, or did he have to hang out in Hold Hell forever like the rest of us? On the other hand, did he even ever need tech support? Probably not. I'm sure he could have gone straight to the top whenever he had a problem. Surely he had a direct line to St. Jude, the patron of impossible causes.

Did he ever get those "you have performed an illegal operation" warnings? Did he worry that *The National Enquirer* might break the story?

What did he do about pornographic spam? Did he simply delete it without opening it, or did he respond and preach to the sender about the evils of sin?

Was he on everyone's jokes mailing list? And did he like the punch line, "Is the pope Catholic?"

As a Catholic myself, I always thought it would be a sure ticket to heaven to get absolution from Mr. Big himself; but getting past the Swiss Guard to see him would have been tricky. Do you suppose he responded to e-mail confessions?

Was he addicted to computer Free Cell solitaire, and did he get annoyed if someone interrupted him midgame? "So? I know there are 50,000 people in the square waiting for midnight Mass, monsignor, but I'm in the middle of my fiftieth straight win. Give me a few minutes, for heaven's sake!"

When he got one of those "fatal error" messages, did he haul out the holy oils and administer the last rites to his computer?

Did he have a separate phone line for his Internet connection, or did his friends have to put up with busy signals when he was online like mine do?

Did he have a digital camera? Did he snap pictures on his travels to e-mail to his buddies?

Did he burn CDs of the Vienna Boys Choir? And did he ever risk breaking copyright infringement laws by downloading music from Napster? If so, did he limit his selections only to songs by Madonna, hoping to hear the first lullaby the Blessed Mother sang in the manger? He may have been curious about how anyone managed to capture her voice long before the technology existed; but since he knew that all things are possible with God, he might have given it a shot. If he did, was he shocked by the Material Girl? Or did he like her? Did he grant her an indulgence electronically for naming her daughter Lourdes?

And, finally, did God really endow John Paul II with infallible wisdom? There was one sure way to find out. Someone should have tested him to see if he could make any sense at all out of his computer manual.

Open, Sesame!

Okay, who's the fiend who dreamed up all the diabolical packaging that plagues us these days? I've searched Google, but no luck. If I could identify the perpetrator, I'd have him (or her) shrinkwrapped and encased in a titanium-strength corrugated, duct-taped carton and airlifted to a desert island, with only a pair of manicure scissors to use as an escape tool.

It all started years ago with childproof caps on medicine bottles, which I am convinced have been solely responsible for sending a multitude of senior citizens off their rockers and into rockers at facilities for the mentally unstable. Dementia? Hardening of the arteries? Depression? No way. It's those damn plastic caps that refuse to turn even when we push down hard as instructed—or at least as hard as we can push now that arthritis has made our hands practically useless. I personally have found a way to keep from going off the deep end trying to open a childproof cap. I simply ask a child to do it for me. Works every time.

And what about those resealable bags that refuse to reseal? You can't tell me that they weren't developed by a gremlin with a macabre sense of humor who cackles gleefully just picturing these bags leaking and spilling their contents all over our refrigerator shelves and cupboards.

As for those ubiquitous Styrofoam peanuts we've all come to

hate, if you're successful in opening any carton containing them, they will immediately explode forth and cover every surface, high and low, including the inaccessible spaces under the piano, the sofa, and beds (yes, they have an uncanny ability to navigate around corners, up and down stairs, and apparently even through closed doors and drawers). Open one of those cartons in your kitchen in January, and you'll still be picking up Styrofoam peanuts when you're searching for your bikini in that old chest in your cellar in July.

And why must so many products, from a small box of paper clips to an eighty-eight-note keyboard, be encased in rigid clear plastic that's stronger than the material used for bank vaults and more form-fitting and unyielding than Scarlett O'Hara's corset? If you don't have a blow torch or an electric saw with a diamond blade, good luck trying to open it.

Then there are those canned products—pet food, sardines, and such—with a metal tab and ring. You're supposed to lift the ring (ha!) and pull it back to remove the top of the can. Who are they kidding? Without a forklift, it's just about impossible. And, let's face it, how many of us have a forklift in our kitchen drawers?

Milk and juice cartons also present a challenge. Unscrewing the cap is easy, but that's just to lull you into a false sense of accomplishment. Once the cap is off, you're faced with a harmless-looking foil circle that's adhered over the pouring spout with a substance that could effectively be used to glue the wings onto the fuselage of a 747.

You have to destroy the carton in order to pour yourself a glass of your morning OJ. By then you desperately need destressing, so you decide to relax to your new *Sounds of Nature* CD. Big mistake. When you finally remove the outer cellophane wrap, after breaking all ten fingernails, can you open the plastic case in which the CD is snugly nestled? Of course not.

Nothing is easily accessible anymore. No wonder I've come to dread the holidays. King Tut's mummy wasn't as tightly wrapped as the cheese log I received last Christmas.

I used to love to see the FedEx guy come, laden with gifts for me. But even in those cute shorts, he has long since lost his appeal. For the past few years, whenever he rang my bell I'd hide, hoping he'd go away; but even if he did, he'd always come back. He was relentless. I finally tried getting a restraining order against him, but the courts refused. Instead, they sent some men in white coats who wrapped me in a straitjacket (more damn packaging!) and took me away.

But please don't send me any get-well gifts. I'll never be able to open them. They don't let me have any sharp instruments here.

Time Flies

More proof that truth is stranger than fiction: physicist Ronald Mallett of the University of Connecticut has actually been working on building a time machine and hopes to have an experimental mockup soon.

No, he's not a crackpot, says he. His studies are solidly based on Einstein's theory of relativity and not on the delusional imaginations of Hollywood scriptwriters or science-fiction authors.

As for me, everything I know about time travel I learned from movies: *Back to the Future,* which was fun and fanciful, and *Kate & Leopold,* which I seriously worried would give some nut the idea that he or she could simply jump off the Brooklyn Bridge and be catapulted into another era.

Can you imagine the implications if Mallett is successful—especially if time travel eventually becomes as accessible as the cross-town bus?

A criminal could flee to another century just before the SWAT team arrives—as could a faithless lover in danger of being found out . . . a kid with a bad report card, afraid to go home . . . a deadbeat dad . . . a mom who can't face one more sink full of dirty dishes. . . . Talk about getting away from it all.

It certainly makes you wonder. If you could pick any moment in time—past or future—which century would you choose?

I'd have to know more than just when. I would also want to

know what my circumstances would be. For example, it might be fun to experience a fashionable soiree in gracious nineteenth-century London—provided I was either the lady of the manor or a well-heeled, noble guest. But with my luck, I'd launch myself to the scene only to find myself in the scullery in midsummer, over a flaming open hearth, roasting suckling pigs for the swells upstairs. Then I could look forward to a morning of mucking out the baronial stables and obeying every other whim of the dictatorial master of the castle. My reward? A few shillings and the promise of even more difficult tasks each day. Come to think of it, that sounds like my first secretarial job.

Or I could book a time-travel trip back to the golden era of luxurious Atlantic crossings on a posh luxury liner, only to see the name *TITANIC* looming down at me as I boarded.

Maybe the future would be a safer bet. After all, we would be assured of not only the technological advantages we enjoy today, but yet more amazing wonders that would astound even Buck Rogers. But how would we choose a date? Again, if my luck runs true to form, I'd select March 16, 2880—the day that the asteroid 1950 DA may very possibly strike Earth.

I wish you the best with your studies, Professor Mallett, but as far as I'm concerned, I think I'll confine my travels to other continents and not other centuries. At least I'll know what I'm dealing with.

And what about Kate, who followed Leopold back to 1876? How long do you think it would take before she'd be hitching a ride back to the twenty-first century? I'm sure I would soon decide that it would be easier to live without handsome Leopold than without automobiles, refrigerators, air conditioning, microwave ovens—and, especially, indoor plumbing. A chamber pot under the bed would really kill the romance.

But maybe that's just me.

Hell on Wheels

Now that I'm retired, what do I miss most about working? The weekly paycheck. What do I miss least? The daily commute to the big city.

For many years I lived twenty miles from my jobs in Boston. Decades ago, one of the steamship lines of the day hyped its leisurely mode of travel with a slogan that proclaimed, "Getting there is half the fun!" This definitely does not apply to commuting to Boston or any metropolis unless you happen to be a sado-masochistic weirdo.

There is no painless (never mind fun-filled) way to get from anywhere to Boston between 6:00 A.M. and noon, a 360-minute span inexplicably called the rush "hour"—singular. The same holds true for the return trip home between 2:00 and 8:00 P.M.

First I tried public transportation. Since I didn't live on the bus line, I had to drive to a rapid-transit station with a parking lot where I left my car and took the trolley into Boston. It was not one of my favorite trips—attested to by the fact that I was never tempted to snap a picture or buy a single souvenir at any of the stops, which is very uncharacteristic of me. Because the trolley was always packed to overcapacity when I boarded, I had to stand, struggling to keep my balance every time we careened around a curve or screeched to a stop. For someone who can't sit in a rocking chair without first taking Dramamine, this was no way to travel.

So I switched to the express turnpike bus, an improvement but hardly Utopia. The fare was higher and, worse, the bus deposited me six blocks from my office. A real disadvantage in winter. To survive the icy winds and subzero temperatures walking from bus to office, I had to dress like Nanook of the North—not the ideal attire for the bus, an overheated sauna on wheels.

Summer was equally traumatic. I had a hard time keeping my cool when the passenger in front of me insisted on opening the window wide, admitting hot blasts of soot-laden air, which blew not only the effects of the air conditioning but also the ten dollars (forty bucks in today's dollars) I had spent at the hairdresser the evening before.

Another problem was that the express bus was the business executives' special. While the trolley crowd read the compact tabloids, the bus riders (at least in public) had a penchant for the *Wall Street Journal* or *New York Times,* oversized papers that infringed on my space. The weaving, darting corners of my seatmate's newspaper continually threatened to dislodge my contacts and/or my corneas, while the top of the paper of the passenger behind me kept ruffling the back of my hair, completing the destruction of my hairdo.

Being young and hopeful at the time, I believed those minor discomforts were a small price to pay for the opportunity to mingle with the passengers—mostly men and mostly affluent, judging from the number of the Mercedes, BMWs, and Volvos in the parking lot. Unfortunately, I soon discovered that my fellow riders were not inclined to fraternize. Speaking to strangers apparently is not encouraged in the tony suburbs. The solution was simple, I thought. The transit company should hire a social director for each trip to provide the necessary proper introductions and to organize mixer-type activities—maybe musical chairs to break the ice while the bus is loading, followed by bowling in the aisle, and maybe even dancing during romantic moments when the bus slows down at the toll booths or plunges into seductively lit tunnels. And, of course, schedules should be arranged to restrict certain runs to singles only. The possibilities are limitless. All that's required is someone with a little imagination to run the transit company.

The first year I commuted to Boston, I kept hoping such a someone would materialize, so I stuck it out—until the holiday shopping season, when all my ho-ho-hos! turned into bah, humbugs! It was impossible to be merry when, exhausted after a long day's work and a twenty-minute trudge through slush and cold, I had to stand up for my return bus trip because the nonworking ladies who had been maxing out their credit cards all day had chosen to wait for the 5:30 bus home. Not only did they appropriate all the seats, but they also staked a claim on every inch of aisle space, plunking their heavy shopping bags smack on the toes of us standees.

That's when I decided that driving my car into the city couldn't possibly be worse. I was wrong, of course. I learned that to hack a path to the city through a solid mass of bumper-to-bumper metal requires nerves of steel. Poor eyesight also helps, because if you can clearly see five lanes of traffic trying to maneuver into the exit ramp you're aiming for, you'll automatically hesitate and you'll be lost—your motor overheating and your gas tank draining dry as you wait in vain for another driver to let you through. They'll find you there in a few years, your bones picked clean by the ever-waiting vultures. (You think that whirling black cloud is smog?)

Of course, another drawback to commuting by automobile was where to put it once I arrived. Because a garage adjoined my office building, finding a parking space wasn't a problem. Finding my car intact at the end of the day, however, was never a certainty. Threading my way through the darkened garage (keeping a wary eye out for potential muggers), I often saw a vehicle that had been vandalized during the day. As I worked, it was not uncommon to hear a shrieking automobile alarm echoing from the adjacent garage. The first time this happened, I panicked—until I remembered that it couldn't be my car. I didn't have an alarm. My relief was short-lived, however, when I thought about that. Then I was nervous whenever I *didn't* hear an alarm.

But the misery of commuting to Boston was compensated for by the pulsating excitement of being there. There are so many fascinating sights in the city! Why, during just one lunch hour, I saw three winos, in picturesque native costume, draped in doorways and gulping their lunch from paper bags; a wild-eyed young man arguing violently with himself and punching the air (until a hapless passerby passed by too closely and inadvertently intercepted the attack); and a placid hippie lying on the curb at a busy intersection with his eyes closed. Was he meditating? Stoned? Or possibly even dead? No one seemed to care. They just stepped over him. As did I, since I didn't dare disobey the traffic signal that ordered, "Walk"—and I was almost picked off by a car whose driver obviously didn't share my respect for traffic signals.

But though I managed to escape being punched out by a disturbed fellow citizen, and I beat the odds of becoming a hit-and-run victim, I still wasn't home free. I almost got high from the ever-present marijuana vapor, I developed what I feared was a terminal wheeze from the exhaust fumes and pollution, and I was almost converted and whisked away by a roving band of saffron-robed Hare Krishnas. I was tempted. Orange is one of my best colors. Furthermore, I would have been happy to shave my head and follow anyone who promised to take me away—preferably to a job in the suburbs.

However, I must admit there are certain educational advantages to working in the big city. For one thing, the graffiti is multilingual.

A short walk of just a couple of blocks is a veritable Berlitz crash course in obscenities—ranging from Arabic to Zulu. And for those who aren't proficient in languages, graphic illustrations are thoughtfully provided as translation aids. In less than a week, I learned that four-letter words don't necessarily have only four letters in other languages. One word I saw appeared to be Italian, but I had never heard it used by any of my relatives. I phoned my mother and asked her what it meant. She reported me to Ma Bell as an obscene caller.

But that's all behind me now. These days, when I feel like working, I commute from my bedroom to my den, where the seat in front of my computer is always available. No crowds, no traffic, no inclement weather, and no graffiti (except on my monitor when I have writer's block and take out my frustration on my keyboard).

Bliss!

Help! I'm a Prisoner in a Moving Vehicle!

I envy intellectuals who ponder weighty questions like: "What is the meaning of life?" "Is there life after death?" "Is God dead?" I don't have time to explore these particular conundrums. I'm much too busy searching for answers to what keeps airplanes up, why doesn't this month's money last until next month's Social Security check, and—most important—where can I park the car?

Compared to this last burning issue, even the reflections of the great philosophers seem insignificant. For example, consider "What is the meaning of life?" If you can't find a parking space, life has no meaning. You can't raise a family, become a Broadway star, or discover a cure for cancer unless you can get out of your car. As for life after death, who knows? I'm not even convinced there's life off the expressway. I do have a theory about God, though. I don't think He's dead. He's probably just double parked somewhere.

I know exactly how He feels, because it often seems that my life revolves around available parking. In fact, an astrologer once told me that the sign with which I am most compatible is *Free Parking*. I don't make plans to be anywhere unless I'm assured a parking space. That's why I never went to a presidential inaugural ball, any of Liz's or Zsa Zsa's weddings, or any A-list bash, for that matter. Not that I've ever been invited, but it's just as well, because I would have had nothing appropriate to wear to any of these events—

again, because of parking problems. There's a great little consignment shop downtown where a worn-just-once designer original costs a fraction of the price of an unimaginative dress jammed on a rack with dozens of duplicates in the department stores of the shopping mall. But though the consignment shop has cheap chic, it doesn't have the mall's parking. So I've resigned myself to spending triple my clothes budget for the privilege of going to a party and seeing clones of my dress on at least two other women and possibly one man, all of whom look prettier in it than I do.

Shopping for groceries is equally frustrating. I don't go to the supermarket that has the best-quality food or the lowest prices. I shop at the one with the largest parking lot. I have similar problems when dining out with friends. Last week it was my turn to drive. I ignored their pleas to go to a favorite restaurant whose chef is a Cordon Bleu graduate and whose owner dropped out of business school the day before the lesson on profit-making. I opted instead for a local eatery where the food is inedible and the prices incredible. "Not the Pit Stop," my friends groaned. "The cook's a part-time mechanic. He uses motor oil in the salad, and his prime ribs taste like Goodyear rejects." "Who cares?" said I. "They have valet parking."

The same insane reasoning prompted me to attend every single Red Sox home game last season. I hate baseball, but a friend who had to be out of town all summer gave me custody of his season's reserved parking space. How could I not take advantage of that?

But all the foregoing is trivial compared to the basic areas of my life that have been shaped solely by available parking. I have no doubt, for instance, that I would have given Neil Simon some stiff competition if it weren't for the fact that there was no parking lot at a city school that offered a great playwriting course. Or, if I found that Broadway wasn't my scene, I could have been president of a major corporation. Unfortunately, whenever I went on job interviews, instead of inquiring about salaries, 401Ks, and promotion possibilities, I asked only about reserved employee parking. Consequently, I had some great parking spaces but some lousy, dead-end jobs.

Not only did I blow my chances of becoming a wealthy, powerful corporate executive, I also passed up every opportunity to marry one. I refused to wed unless the ceremony included a promise by the groom to park my car until death do us part, and they all balked at that. I would have even turned down Paul Newman in his prime, unless he swore he wouldn't give Joanne custody of the driveway and garage.

If Prince Charming had ever shown up with a crystal slipper large enough to fit me, I would have turned him down, too. How could I have adjusted to life in a castle? With all those surrounding moats, the closest parking is probably two acres beyond the jousting field.

But I exaggerate. Back in the real world of the common folk, if you really must find a parking space, you can always resort to a garage or commercial lot—if you're independently wealthy. As for me, even if I could afford the exorbitant fees, I would avoid the lots and garages that require you to give your keys to a sixteen-year-old reject from the Indy 500 who will try to carom your five-foot-wide car into a four-foot-wide space. Of course, some garages don't require you to leave your keys. You can park your car yourself. However, when you come back to retrieve it, it's jammed behind six rows of other vehicles, all belonging to swingers who aren't going home until dawn, so neither are you.

It's all very stressful. I try to relax . . . to stop and smell the roses. Unfortunately, they're all growing in No Parking zones.

Flash! I just heard a bulletin on my car radio. It has been confirmed that God is not dead. My theory was not far wrong. He's not double parked, but a Roman traffic helicopter just spotted Him circling St. Peter's Square (pretty tricky, even for God) looking for a parking space.

Foolish Fashion

When I was young (wasn't that yesterday?), every female between six months and 106 was supposed to believe that fashion was fun. I bought into that nonsense for years. Now, however, I've become a traitor to my sex. As far as I'm concerned, the whole fashion scene is a rip-off.

It feels so good to admit that—to finally come out of the closet—a closet jammed with inappropriate, unattractive, unflattering creations foisted on me over the years by saleswomen who insisted, "But honey, that dress [jumpsuit, boa, bikini] is you!" Months later, when it was too late to return them, I realized that not only were they not me, they weren't even anyone I'd care to know.

As I grew older and wiser, when salespeople couldn't convince me I looked ravishing in baggy burlap, stressed denim, or see-through stretch lace, they tried instead to impress me with an article's pedigree. "But it's a genuine copy of Dior's adaptation of Givenchy's latest!" Who cares? As a child, I objected to my mother telling me what to eat and my father telling me what time to come home. So now that I'm well beyond even my second childhood, why should I let a bunch of strangers tell me what to wear just because they speak French and have fancy addresses on the Rue Honoré? If the only attractive feature about an article of clothing is its label, do I really want it?

I long ago decided it shouldn't be necessary to pay more for clothes than it used to cost to send your kid to college. I took a good look around and found lots of women who spend less on attire than the average six-year-old blows on Barbie's spring wardrobe, yet they always look smashing. I finally figured out their secret. They have a knack for buying a simple shirt . . . a scarf . . . a piece of costume jewelry . . . all of which coordinate beautifully with everything else they own and tie it all chicly together.

"I can do that," I figured. I was wrong.

After spending my vacation fund and a week in the boutiques (instead of Martinique as I had planned), I ended up with a collection of accessories that didn't quite make it with anything I owned. That beautifully simple blouse was a little too simple for my dressier pants and just a hair off-color for any of my plaids or tweeds. That unusual stickpin that looked so elegant and tasteful in the store screamed, *"Tacky!"* the minute I took it out of its box at home. And the signature scarf I chose stubbornly refused to coordinate with anything else in my wardrobe. Furthermore, the signature was illegible.

Naturally, I didn't discover these defects until I had thrown away all the receipts. Unfortunately, I didn't throw in the towel (even though it was last season's color and not even monogrammed). Instead, I went shopping again—this time to try to find outfits to showcase my new accessories. My timing was perfect. I hit all the end-of-season sales. No returns, but such bargains! Except that when I got my new slacks home, they weren't any more compatible with that independent blouse I had bought than were any of my old trousers. My new coat, which really cried for a splash of color, cried even louder when confronted with the particular hues of my signature scarf. And the neckline of my new dress just wasn't the right foil for my hideous stickpin . . . yet it needed something. . . .

I had an epiphany. I decided I would no longer be a slave to the fashion gurus. What do they know? Women who follow designers' dictums, striving to look provocative, more often wind up looking pathetic.

Consider the "peasant look" that keeps making a comeback every few years. Those off-the-shoulder blouses that look so sensational on voluptuous damsels of sixteen lose a great deal in the translation to the fifty-and-flabby set, who insist on wearing them because *Vogue* so decrees. As a result, a stranger arriving on our shores must think we've been invaded by a horde of fat gypsy matrons.

This sort of thing is so unnecessary. Designers are perfectly capable of turning out mature, sophisticated styles. The only problem is that they're turning them out only in sizes 6 months to 6X. I ask you, does any three-year-old really need black leather pants and a matching tank top? Of course not—no more than a sixty-year-old dowager needs ruffles and puffed sleeves. But thanks to the fashion designers, our planet is overrun with preschool seductresses and aging ingénues. I'm not proposing that any kid should show up for kindergarten wearing Pampers, mind you; and neither do I think that Whistler's mother should have looked so drab for her portrait—after all, it wasn't as if she'd been caught off-guard by "Candid Camera." All I'm saying is that we should use some common sense.

To this end, I've drawn up a few guidelines.

• Anyone old enough to cross the street without holding Mommy's hand is too old to wear ribbons in her hair.

• Although a little pot belly is adorable on a tiny tot, it loses its charm when it's fifty-plus years old and is hanging over a skimpy bikini.

• The only time leotards should be worn to exercise class is on graduation day, after you've achieved your goal of a perfect figure.

• Even though a new style may be "with it," you may be better off without it.

• Shoes that require you to check your accident policy and notify your next of kin prior to wearing are a no-no.

• Never buy clothes that are really "today." If you're going to shell out a few hundred dollars for an outfit, you should also be able to wear it tomorrow.

• Avoid T-shirts with risqué sayings printed on them unless you want nearsighted strangers with bad breath sidling up to read your bosom.

Let's put an end to fashion tyranny! Picket *Vogue*'s offices! Storm Seventh Avenue! Form protest marches against all the fancy-schmancy stores!

I'd join you, but I really don't have anything appropriate to wear.

Sex–Then and Now

I'm confused. I know times have changed—but this much?

Someone recently wrote in to a gossip column to ask if a certain actress ever married her longtime actor fiancé. "Not yet" was the response. "Every time we plan a wedding," said she, "I seem to get pregnant." Hello?! Didn't pregnancy used to be a good reason to *get* married—not to postpone it?

A book I read a while back, *In the Deep Midwinter,* by Robert Clark, published in 1997 but set in the 1940s, is a strong reminder of the way things used to be. Anna loves Charles, who is about to propose. She would be deliriously happy—except for one problem. She suspects she is pregnant with his child, and she is certain that when she tells Charles, he will immediately dump her. "He'll think I'm cheap!" she wails to her friend Alice. Am I missing something here? Anna apparently feels that the fact that she has been sleeping with Charles for months has not diminished her in his eyes, but now that she's pregnant because she forgot to use her diaphragm once or twice, he'll think she's a slut. Huh?

I grew up in Anna's era, and I would have written her off as a "bad" girl way before the pregnancy. She would have landed on my blacklist just by making out with Charles the first time. Of course, back then I really didn't know what "making out" meant. First, second, and third base? They were just markers on a ball field. To me, "sex" simply defined gender. I was beyond naive. I was probably legally able to vote before I was certain that the stork really didn't bring babies. For a while I thought pregnancy resulted from something called "French kissing," whatever that was. I had no clue. I just knew that a boy had to be involved and that any girl who had a baby before she was married was beyond redemption, doomed to hell—and her family disgraced forever.

It happened to only one of my high-school classmates, or so the story went. No one ever actually knew for a fact, but she did gain a lot of weight and then suddenly left school to "visit" an aunt 2,000 miles away. She never returned. Rumors flew. Did she have a baby? Did she keep it? Who was the father? Did he marry her? Of course not. Back then boys did not marry "that kind of girl." He probably admitted his paternity at some point, however. Why? Not because DNA tests precluded a denial, but because he was proud of his sexual prowess. His reputation wasn't ruined. On the contrary, it was enhanced. There was definitely something wrong with that picture.

Women's lib changed all that. Nowadays, both sexes, young as well as old, are publicly promiscuous without risking disapproval. They even brag about it in the press and on national television. Single motherhood? Hey, that's now a badge of honor. Leading the trend are celebrities who are praised for their selflessness. On the other hand, anyone over fifteen who is courageous enough to admit to being a virgin is ridiculed. She/he is considered to be either hopelessly unattractive, frigid, or saddled with preposterously outdated hang-ups. Even younger children who may not yet be "going all the way" are certainly well on the way. I heard on a television talk show last week that oral sex is a favorite pastime of middle-school kids across America. Really? Whatever happened to tag . . . hide and seek . . . hopscotch . . . ? Remember when kids used to get their mouths washed out with soap for saying a naughty word? What's the punishment for oral sex? A scouring with industrial-strength Ajax?

I admit that my generation was probably too inhibited. The raciest thing we ever saw on television were Rob and Laura Petrie's twin beds on "The Dick Van Dyke Show." But I think we were happier than today's youth, who are supposedly freer but pressured on all sides to engage in so-called adult behavior long before they're ready. And when they do reach maturity, having already experienced it all, they're jaded, disillusioned, and depressed. Fidelity? Responsibility? What a drag. It's not surprising that older husbands turn to Viagra and nymphets, while their wives resort to botox and breast implants in order to seduce boy toys. Of course, it helps if they can bait their beds with money and gifts, because if today's boys and girls just want sex, they don't need older partners. They can get plenty of action in school.

It gives a whole new meaning to the term "playground."

Confessions of a Lowbrow

The secret's out: I am hopelessly uncouth . . . unsophisticated
. . . uncultured . . . unrefined.

Primary evidence of my lack of taste is my addiction to television sitcoms. As is the case with most vile habits, I acquired
this shameful craving in my youth. I blush to admit it, but I
couldn't get through one week without my Dick Van Dyke fix.
And soon that wasn't enough. I had to have more. Before long, I
was gripped by an obsessive passion for Mary Tyler Moore, Bob
Newhart, Murphy Brown, the entire M*A*S*H cast, and—heav-
en help me—Archie Bunker.

When these shows ended, I suffered tormenting withdrawal
symptoms. Yet somewhere deep inside, I realized that it was for
the best. I could finally get that monkey off my back. But no.
Soon I got sucked back into all the spin-offs—"Rhoda,"
"Phyllis," "The Jeffersons," "Golden Girls"—followed by the
spin-offs of the spin-offs, to say nothing of the reruns of the original series and all their offshoots.

Then came "Cheers," "Seinfeld," "Mad About You," "Will &
Grace" . . . so much temptation, so little willpower. I gave up trying to fight. Consequently, even today I keep the *TV Guide* next
to my calendar to ensure that I don't make any social plans that
conflict with my dates with "The King of Queens" and the gang
at "The Office."

In my defense, I'm still trying to kick the habit. I don't watch sitcoms exclusively. I'm a longtime fan of "Jeopardy" (who says I'm not intellectual?); and I developed a mania for "The West Wing," whose cast was almost as entertaining as their real counterparts in Washington. I also occasionally stray to the reality shows—"Survivor," "The Apprentice," "Fear Factor." . . . But I still have a long way to go to match the standards of all my friends who view only CNN or PBS. Not to brag, but I also watch PBS occasionally. (Okay, I admit it, the British sitcoms.)

And my indiscriminate taste isn't limited to TV. I love the theater, for example, but give me a comedy (where have you gone, Neil Simon?) or a good old musical any time. Unfortunately, they don't make 'em like they used to . . . *South Pacific; My Fair Lady; Mame; Hello, Dolly!* . . . I even loved *Kiss Me Kate* and *West Side Story,* despite the fact that they were based on Shakespearean plays; so maybe I'm not completely hopeless.

Or maybe I am. I apparently sank to new lows during a recent trip to the Big Apple. No, I didn't join the ladies of the evening on Times Square. Worse. I engaged in hick-from-the-sticks touristy activities. In fact, one morning I actually went to Rockefeller Center to watch "Today." One of my friends was appalled when she heard about it. Rolling her eyes and shaking her head, she tsked, "You did that?!" What she doesn't know is that if I had had access to any crafts materials in my hotel, I would have made and worn a crazy hat to catch the attention of the cameraman. Is there no limit to my depravity?

Furthermore, I do not subscribe to the *New York Times, Wall Street Journal,* or *U.S. News & World Report.* However, neither do I read *The Enquirer, The Star,* or other tabloids. But then, nobody does—right? All we confess to is a quick glance at the headlines as we pass through the checkout aisle at the supermarket. Did you know that Elvis is alive and planning to run for president? (If the aliens who are invading next week don't get to him first.)

Since I've come this far, I may as well also admit that I can't tell the difference between a $500 bottle of fine wine and the stuff in a jug with a screw top, or between Starbucks' best and decaf instant coffee. Also, I love the Boston Pops, but the Boston Symphony, not so much. In fact, when I was dragged to a recent performance, I thought the musicians were tuning their instruments but they were playing Penderecki's *Threnody for the Victims of Hiroshima.* I guarantee that's something not even the most cultured among us will be humming on their way out of the hall.

I don't shop at Saks, Bloomingdales, Neiman Marcus, or even Macy's. No, my retailer of choice is an establishment called Frugal Fannie's.

I could continue this confession and reveal still darker secrets, but I have to go. My *TV Guide* says it's time for "Two and a Half Men."

Give Me the Simple Life

Is it my imagination, or is life becoming increasingly complicated every day? Didn't everything used to be a lot simpler?

Remember the old telephones, for example? They came in one model only—a black, clunky, two-piece job with a separate mouthpiece and earpiece. No decisions to make. No choice of designs or colors. And all were connected to our homes or offices through a network of cables. Only Dick Tracy had a wireless phone (in his wristwatch, as I recall), but that was strictly science fiction. None of us actually believed that someday we would be walking around with tiny cell phones, calling home from the car or from the toilet-paper aisle of the supermarket to ask if we should buy the brand that's on sale or the expensive, super-soft rolls. As a matter of fact, back then, we didn't have supermarkets. Just the corner grocer. And he didn't have to ask which brand of tushy tissue we wanted. There was only one.

And remember telephone operators? When you wanted to make a phone call, you'd lift the earpiece off the hook of the old black phone, and a friendly real person would ask, "Number, please?" Then she (never he) would connect you directly to the party you were calling. After a few rings, another friendly voice would reply. Again, an actual human being—not a recording offering you a dozen menu choices. It was amazing.

Even more miraculous, when you phoned your doctor, you

could actually speak to him (seldom her). I could even call my doctor at home at 3:00 A.M. back then. Not anymore. Today, I reach a voicemail system and eventually a secretary, who relays my concerns to the doctor and gets back to me in a day or two with the doctor's response. At least that's what I'm led to believe. I sometimes wonder if my doctor actually exists, or is this whole message-relay business merely a scam to give me a false sense of security? Maybe the secretary just goes on the Internet, does a Google search on my question, and then calls me back with her own advice. Of course, I do see my doctor in person when I go for my annual physical—or do I? For all I know she could be a computer-programmed hologram.

As for all the medical insurance paperwork, what's that about? We never used to have to get tangled in miles of red tape. And how come though we have all kinds of expensive insurance coverage, we still end up coughing up tons of additional money for every visit, procedure, and prescription?

Then there's the automobile. I remember three auto makers in my childhood—Ford, Chevrolet, and Chrysler. Each manufactured only two or three models in two or three colors. The only place you could buy a foreign car was in a foreign land—which really wasn't an option, since only a handful of Americans had enough money to travel abroad. Today, of course, we can choose from a staggering number of automobile manufacturers, domestic and foreign, each of which turns out a multitude of different models in myriad colors. It's a smorgasbord of expensive excess.

Repairs are another modern nightmare. Before, when the old Chevy, Ford, or Chrysler didn't work right, Joe, the mechanic down the street, could tell immediately that the thingamajig connecting the whatchamacallit to the whosiwhatsit was broken. He'd replace it for a few bucks and you were back on the road. Today you must bring your car to a state-of-the-art facility, where you wait interminably, sipping cappuccino, while a dozen specialists consult and conduct diagnostic electronic tests to determine which computer chip is malfunctioning; and you're obliged to take out a second mortgage on your house to pay for the repair. Speaking of houses, my parents bought a beautiful home when I was a child for one-third the price of my last new car, and my car doesn't even have indoor plumbing. I wouldn't be surprised if that's coming next.

Another aspect of modern life that is definitely more complicated today is raising children, especially when they become adolescents. It's not their fault. Apparently Congress passed a law when we weren't paying attention that requires kids to become obnoxious at the onset of puberty. They absolutely must rebel against Mom and Dad in order to "separate," the psychiatrists tell us. It's a healthy rite of passage. Really? How come my generation managed to make it to adulthood by remaining docile through our teens? Nobody told us we were supposed to rant and rave, pierce our navels, nipples, and noses, dye our hair purple, tattoo our bodies, and hate our parents. Yet we survived. Furthermore, we didn't revolt even though we were cruelly denied designer clothes, a closet full of hundred-dollar sneakers, and our own cars at sixteen. Hey, my parents didn't even own a car when I was sixteen. We walked everywhere—to school, to the movies, to shops, to church. . . . Consequently, we were in much better shape than most people today, even though expensive gyms and personal trainers were unheard of.

Furthermore, when I was a kid, the only labels on my clothes said *Irregular,* and my shoe wardrobe consisted of a pair of cloth Keds for play, a pair of loafers for school, and a pair of Mary-Janes for Sunday school. Such deprivation would probably be considered child abuse in this "enlightened" age.

Remember when we'd get together with the neighborhood kids after supper (one that Mom actually cooked—not a Happy Meal) and played Red Rover, Kick the Can, and stickball? Kids don't do that anymore. Their "play" is now rigidly structured and competitive. They go to gymnastics classes, they vie for starting positions on school soccer and basketball teams, and they struggle with little league baseball and hockey—too often with coaches and parents on the sidelines loudly exhorting them to excel. They have to be stars. They're pressured to prove they're smarter/faster/more talented than all the other kids. Unfortunately, simply having fun is no longer an option for most of today's kids. Stress has become the name of the game.

It's not surprising that many of them rebel when they grow tall enough to intimidate their parents. They're not "separating"—they're getting even.

Our Special Guest Today Is . . .

Has anyone besides me noticed that all the TV talk shows now consist almost entirely of commercials? The usual paid product advertising is interrupted every few minutes by interviews with celebrities touting their latest book, movie, TV show, CD, or exercise video. And if you miss them on "Today," you can catch them an hour later on "Live with Regis and Kelly." They just dash from one studio to the next, usually without even bothering to change their clothes, their hype, or their film clips. And within a week, they'll be shamelessly pitching on "Good Morning America," "The Early Show," and "Oprah," followed by late-night chats with David and Jay . . . sales of their products soaring with each appearance.

Of course, if I could get equal time, this whole process wouldn't bother me one bit. But since I can't, I think it's a lousy system. (Does a heaping bowl full of sour grapes count as one of my daily fruit servings?)

Why do I deserve to get in on all the fanfare? Because I have written some wonderful children's books. Really. Gen, my schoolteacher friend, read them to her first-grade class—a notoriously tough audience—and she reported that not one of them made a face or gagged. Hey, that's high praise from that crowd.

Unfortunately, my books have been rejected more often than a guy with roast beef on his breath at a vegetarian's convention, even though many publishers returned them with letters filled with lavish praise. (*Your story is charming . . . reminiscent of Dr. Seuss . . . delightfully imaginative. . . .*) Unfortunately, the praise was always followed by regret. (*Sorry, but we are in the process of publishing a similar story. . . . We have received 20,000 submissions for the year to date, from which we have chosen the 3 we will publish. . . . Our budget does not allow us to gamble with an unknown writer. . . .*)

That's me, an unknown writer—not a celebrity like so many so-called authors who are producing children's books these days. It's that old vicious circle. No one will promote me because I'm not famous; and I can't become famous unless someone promotes me

Does Katie Couric care? Are Regis and Kelly bombarding me with calls, begging me to appear on their show? Will Oprah ever offer me a seat on her couch?

Oops! There's the phone. Maybe it's Barbara Walters, inviting me to appear on "The View."

Right. And next week I'm flying to Rome to become pope.

Diet Is a Four-Letter Word

Diet is a four-letter word, the first three of which spell something many people would almost prefer to do rather than deprive themselves of the four basic foods: pastry, pasta, potato chips, and potent potables.

Have you wondered why obesity is such a huge (so to speak) problem in America despite the proliferation of diet books? Maybe it's *because* of those diet books, which have spawned a whole generation of diet-a-week fanatics. I'm one myself. Every Sunday I read about the latest miracle program, resolve to start it the next morning, and then spend the rest of the day gorging, convinced it's perfectly okay because, after all, I'm beginning a diet tomorrow. Oh, the pounds we gain on Sunday in anticipation of the diet we're starting on Monday.

It's a shame that no one has created positive PR to convince us that starving is fun. It's not so farfetched. Look what the advertising honchos did for smoking all those years. No one actually enjoyed that first cigarette, what with all the gasping, choking, and throwing up. But most people stuck with it and forced themselves to get used to it because the ads made it so glamorous. The subliminal message was that if you smoked, you too would be one of the beautiful people (instead of one of the dead ones).

So why can't dieting, which is good for us, be made as appealing as was smoking, which is bad for us? One problem is that cutting calories devastates your social life. Everything we do today revolves around food and booze: "Meet me downtown for a drink. . . . " "Let's get together for dinner next week. . . . " "How about coming over for a game of Scrabble?" (which you'll play if you can find the board under the plates of goodies on the table).

You go to visit friends, and before you have your coat off, a martini has been shoved into one hand and a potato chip dripping sour-cream dip in the other—presumably to give you enough energy to make it to the sofa and sit down, smack in front of the coffee table laden with cocktail frankfurters, mini pizzas, liver paté, a variety of cheeses, and enough assorted nuts to supply all the bars in five counties for a month. Mind you, these are just the appetizers to start your digestive juices flowing for a seven-course meal, topped off by seven-layer cake and a choice of seven after-dinner liqueurs.

Invariably, after a long period of such binge eating, I go to the other extreme. My diets make Mahatma Gandhi's fasts look like Henry VIII's feasts. But before long, I weaken, and when I lose my willpower, I become a closet eater. I have the irrational belief that if no one sees me scarfing down that platter of fettuccine Alfredo, I won't get fat. Who am I kidding? I know very well that the Great Calorie Counter in the Sky totes up every milligram and sees to it that the balance is deposited on my hips, with interest, by dawn.

Nevertheless, I can always find excuses to break my diet. There's a terrible storm, thunder makes me tense, and tension makes me eat. . . . I'm so relieved when the weatherman reports that the worst is over, and relief makes me hungry. . . . I'm working hard and must eat to keep up my energy. . . . I'm on vacation, and you can't diet while on vacation (doesn't it say so in the Bill of Rights?). . . .

And it's not much better for me at home, unless I keep the cupboard and refrigerator bare. There is no way a gallon of ice cream or a blueberry pie can ever have a long shelf life (like, say, fifteen minutes) in my house. I don't even have to be hungry. Until it's all gone, I won't rest. After the first helping, I don't even enjoy it, but I keep devouring it. Why? Because, like Mount Everest, it's there. I don't know which is worse—the guilt or the nausea.

A friend of mine was dieting and doing quite well. When I saw him a month later, it was apparent that he had regained the pounds he had lost, and more. "What happened?" I asked. "I had a terrible accident," he moaned. I was all sympathy, picturing him in traction, getting no exercise and being force-fed high-caloric milkshakes to provide enough calcium for his bones to knit. "Turnpike?" I asked. "Kitchen," he replied. "I slipped and fell in front of the refrigerator, the door flew open, and before I could save myself, a pound of pastrami and a quart of chocolate ice cream fell into my mouth . . . for starters."

Just listening to him made me hungry. So as an antidote, I immediately picked up a magazine whose cover touted the latest "painless" diet. Unfortunately, it was one of those publications where you need a table of contents to find the table of contents. Before I located the diet article, I had drooled my way through a ten-page, full-color spread of the most luscious looking desserts since Satan invented strawberry cheesecake. It was all over—again.

I headed for the refrigerator. . . .

But it's okay. I'm starting a new diet tomorrow.

Have You Ever Had One of Those Days?

Last week when my car's fuel gauge read *Empty* and I was in a hurry, I decided to pay at the pump. I think my credit card choked on the price of the gas and self-destructed, because it never reemerged. At least I hope it died and didn't float out to cyberspace, where a hacker snatched it and is now enjoying a luxurious all-expenses-paid (by me) romp around the world.

It all started when I got up that morning, stubbed my toe on the bathroom door frame, and glanced at the mirror. Disaster! I've had more bad hair days than a gaggle of punk rockers, but this morning's "do" made those others look positively chic by comparison.

Ignoring the omen, I showered (no hot water!), dressed (how did that shirt get so wrinkled in my closet?), and left in a torrential downpour for a round of errands. My first stop was to the drugstore for batteries—two packs for the price of one, this week only. They were sold out. Surprise. I had to wait ten minutes until a fruitless backroom search produced no cache of batteries and a rain check was eventually proffered. I then handed the cashier (a young recruit-in-training) another ad for a "twofer" deal of the week—multivitamins. Both bottles rang in at full price. A lengthy, high-level managerial conference eventually rectified that problem. But it didn't end there. The adorable little teddy bear I had picked up on a whim as a gift for my grandnephew refused to reveal its price, despite the cashier's multiple desperate scans of its bar code. At this point, I was sure she was seriously questioning her career choice and wondering if she wouldn't be happier elsewhere asking, "Would you like to supersize that?"

My next stop was the drive-up ATM at the bank. Sheets of rain sluiced into the overhang that was futilely trying to protect the machine. I was thankful that I had pulled up close enough to conduct my transaction without having to get out of the car. I punched in a withdrawal request. Usually I have to yank the bills out of the slot, which never gives them up without a struggle. This time, however, five twenties exploded from the contraption. A spray of green zipped past my hand and hit the puddled pavement in all directions. And because I had driven smack up against the ATM to avoid getting wet, I couldn't open my car door. I had to pull ahead and then leap out to retrieve the scattered, sodden bills before they were whirled to Oz with the next gust of wind. But at least I wasn't worried about my hair. It couldn't possibly look any worse than it did when I left home.

The post office was my next destination. Four of the five windows were unattended, and the only clerk on duty was serving a customer. Fortunately, I was next. I waited patiently for several minutes, and then waited *im*patiently for many more as a line grew behind me and the gentleman in front of me at the window showed no signs of completing his business. He wondered what special stamps were available. The clerk showed him several choices. He pondered them carefully. "Are these the only ones?" he asked. "Maybe we have more," she said cheerfully. "I'll check." She disappeared, then returned a few minutes later laden with folders that she spread on the counter before him. "Oh, look!" said he. "This one says, 'Happy Birthday'! That's nice. Hmmm . . . I like this pelican . . . but maybe the flowers . . . ? I'm not sure which ones my wife would prefer. . . . " She understood perfectly and smiled sweetly, offering alternate suggestions, until he finally made a choice. He paid her. She gave him change. Still standing at the window, he carefully—and slowly—stowed it in his wallet, put the wallet in his pocket, and then—equally carefully and slowly—folded up his stamps and put them in another pocket. Oblivious to the growing groans from the throng behind him, he and the clerk then exchanged leisurely farewell pleasantries as he stooped to pick up his umbrella and two bags of groceries he had put on the floor. He started to leave. But before I could claim the window, he turned. "Wait!" he said. "Maybe I'll take a few of those Cary Grant stamps, too. My wife will like those. . . . " "Oh, I'm sure she will!" enthused the clerk, who was much too young to have any idea who Cary Grant was. "And maybe some of the flowers," continued the man as he set down his packages and pulled out his wallet again. . . .

One would think I'd had enough at that point and gone straight home. But no. I decided to stop at the supermarket, just for milk. It would be quick. Unfortunately, apparently everyone in town had realized that they, too, were out of milk. The nearest available parking space was on the outer fringe of the vast lot. And, of course, the rain was still cascading like Niagara Falls. But I really did need that milk. I got out of the car, waded to the market, and went directly to the dairy case, leaving lake-size puddles in my wake. I grabbed a quart of 2 percent instead of my usual skim (hey, I needed *some* solace after all I'd been through) and headed for the checkout lanes. I pondered anew why all these stores boast at least sixteen cash registers but never seem to have more than three in operation. I joined the shortest of the three lines. Big mistake. The woman in front of me, who was buying only a candy bar, had nothing but a hundred-dollar bill. The clerk had to page a manager for authorization. He was on a coffee break—apparently in Colombia with Juan Valdez, judging from the time it took him to respond. The cashier then discovered she didn't have enough money in her drawer to make change. Another emergency page for help. No response. Maybe it had to be delivered by Brinks? She smiled apologetically and paged again. . . .

Meanwhile, in the other two lanes, shoppers whose carts overflowed with enough supplies to furnish the next five Everest expeditions were being speedily processed and sent on their way.

I abandoned my milk and fled—to the liquor store next door. Two percent milk was not going to fill the solace bill.

I have a new favorite ad slogan: "Got scotch?"

How Mickey Mouse Saved My Life–and Vice Versa

I knew I had an obsession with food decades ago when I suddenly realized that the main reason I was looking forward to a movie starring Paul Newman (who was absolutely gorgeous back then) was because it would give me an excuse to inhale an industrial-size bucket of popcorn (with extra butter).

That was a sure sign I needed professional help; and since I couldn't afford a personal nutritionist or a shrink, I decided to join a weight-loss group. My mother was horrified when she heard the news. Better I should have announced I was entering the world's oldest profession. "If you want to kill yourself," she said, "why don't you just slash your wrists? It's quicker." We couldn't discuss it further because she had to leave to plan my funeral.

In Mom's defense, I must explain that she wasn't a fat faddist who thought everyone needs at least twenty extra pounds to ward off the plague. It's just that she never got over my scrawny childhood, when I was the world's finickiest eater and she was convinced I would die of malnutrition before my fifth birthday. I would have made Morris the cat look like a glutton, except he wasn't around until later, when he achieved fame in TV commercials for refusing to nibble anything except the sponsor's overpriced gourmet cat food.

Mickey Mouse *was* around back then, though, which was

fortunate, because he saved my life. It seems I wouldn't swallow a morsel until Mom convinced me that Mickey would be devastated and die of sorrow unless I took "just one more bite." Telling me that children in Africa were starving did not induce me to eat. I could never understand how my cleaning my plate would help them. And frankly, I secretly envied them not having to deal with eating. They were faceless, anonymous. But Mickey Mouse was a different story. Mickey was my friend. I knew him. I loved him. I would have done anything in my power not to hurt him.

You must understand that this was a long time before Mickey was luxuriating at his palatial palaces in Disneyland and Disney Worlds around the globe. Back then he was just a poor little creature who only made a weekly appearance in the Sunday funnies. With not much going for him, he seemed very vulnerable; and I truly believed that if I didn't please him by eating at least some of my breakfast, lunch, and dinner, he would pine away from sadness. (Hey, that's what my mother said. Would she lie?)

Well, Mickey survived, and so did I. I grew older and less picky (i.e., I would eat anything that didn't move) and, inevitably, heavier. That damn mouse did too good a job! But Mom (and everyone else) still perceived me as skinny because my thin face belied the excess padding on the rest of my bones. So she wasn't really worried about what she considered my ridiculous plan to join the weight-loss club. She was certain they wouldn't even let me in the door. "They'll take one look at you and laugh," she predicted. She was mistaken. Nobody even snickered. They told me to lose seventeen pounds. It was a struggle, but I did it. And much to my mother's surprise, I didn't fade away and die. She never came out and admitted she was wrong; but after that, whenever I went to dinner, she didn't set the Mickey Mouse plate at my place.

Unfortunately, it's been a long time since I needed any urging whatsoever to devour anything put in front of me. On the contrary, instead of begging me to eat "just one more bite" for Mickey Mouse, maybe someone should have given me an incentive *not* to clean my plate—like promising me a date with Paul Newman (I told you—he really was gorgeous back then). Today, though, that wouldn't work. Like me, Paul is older (and not quite so gorgeous), and my priorities have changed.

These days I'd rather have a super-sized hot-fudge sundae. (Sorry, Paul.) And don't be stingy with the whipped cream.

How to Put Off Until Never What You Should Have Done Last Week

Procrastination has such a bad reputation. Undeservedly so. Think about it. Those who do not procrastinate never have time to enjoy themselves, even after a hard day's work at the day job. They're always too busy obeying that nagging voice in their heads that keeps reminding them of the bills to be paid . . . the phone calls to return . . . the beds to make . . . the floors to wash . . . the kids' homework to check . . . the errands to run . . . the checkbook to balance . . . the toilets to scrub. . . . These poor suckers complete one task, and a dozen others demand attention. The doers never catch up. Their only hope is to learn the ancient art of procrastination.

Yes, ancient. Procrastination originated in Eden, you see, when Eve was propositioned by a snake in the grass who promised to put her on the cover of the first issue of *Vogue* in exchange for her soul. Tempted by the prospect of fame and fortune as the universe's first top model, she nagged Adam to gather some flax and weave her a suitably chic outfit. But Adam kept saying, "Maybe later."

In reality, Adam was no slouch. And no fool. He simply preferred Eve in her birthday suit. Furthermore, he knew if he spent all day weaving, he wouldn't have time to do the things he enjoyed—such as taking bites from Eve's apple, which he may not have been inclined to do had she been wrapped in flax.

Unfortunately, early historians erroneously blamed the couple's eviction from Eden, not on Eve's avarice and lust for fame, but on Adam's delay in granting her unreasonable demand. And so it came to pass that "procrastination" became a dirty word, a misconception that has persisted throughout the ages.

In the prehistoric centuries that followed, there was little need for anyone to emulate Adam's delaying tactics, because people had very few obligations. No Rotary Club meetings, no office hours, no church services, no dentist appointments . . . No one could read or write, so "To Do" lists were unknown.

In short, during that period there was seldom any incentive to practice procrastination, except for occasional exceptions such as when the family got hungry and the wife would nag her napping husband to go kill dinner. Even though the caveman had never learned about Adam, an atavistic impulse would kick in, and he'd grunt, "Ugh$#%@&!" ("Maybe later!")

Procrastination really came into its own when the Greeks discovered democracy. As we all know, legislative bodies never get anything done. This same period, according to historians, spawned the empty promises, "I'll take care of it" and "The check is in the mail."

Later, during the Renaissance, schools proliferated, the arts blossomed, literature flourished, and accomplishment became a prime goal—further challenging man's ingenuity to find ways to avoid responsibility. Take, for example, Michelangelo's painting of the Sistine Chapel ceiling. It is a recorded fact that when he submitted his estimate, he promised, "A year, eighteen months at the outside, counting pasta breaks." But one thing led to another, and before the Vatican VIPs realized it, thirty years had passed and Mickey still hadn't completed the job.

Other notable procrastinators include Scarlett O'Hara, who lived by the philosophy, "I'll think about that tomorrow," and Hamlet, who kept putting off his decision of whether to be or not to be.

Thousands of other fictional and real slackers through the years understood that one of the prime benefits of procrastination is ego gratification. They realized that if you actually tackle a project and botch it, there's no turning back. Everyone will know you failed. On the other hand, if you keep putting a job off, you can tell yourself (and everyone else) that you could do it brilliantly—if you had the time. Maybe later.

Most people have been brainwashed to believe that procrastinators are lazy clods. Not so. We are constantly busy, but only with activities we fancy, rather than the unpleasant, boring tasks that society tries to impose on us. In truth, procrastinators lead rich, full lives that lack only the three Ds: drudgery, duty, and deadlines.

The conscientious accomplisher, on the other hand, ruled by these same three Ds, never has time for R&R, even when he has completed a difficult task. Because the sooner and the better he does it, the more in demand he is for the next job waiting to be done. Once on that treadmill, the harder he runs, the faster he generates more work for himself. Because of the lack of proper education in this area, too many unfortunates trudge this treadmill of accomplishment from infancy to senility, never once tasting the joys of procrastination.

Why has the plight of this miserable majority been ignored? Certainly not for lack of good intentions. In fact, thousands of studies of this international tragedy have been initiated over the centuries. Unfortunately, not one has ever been completed. You can help by demanding legislative action to create head-start programs to help the disadvantaged—those unfortunate over-achievers, the compulsive go-getters. Write your congressman today . . . or tomorrow . . . next month . . . whenever you get around to it. In fact, you can use thinking about writing that letter as an excuse for putting off an even more distasteful task, like cleaning the roof gutters or changing the baby.

Meanwhile, why not visit a bookstore? Just think of the wonderfully unproductive hours you can spend, purposelessly browsing the aisles, flipping through the latest bestsellers, travel tomes, cookbook collections, and so much more. Be scrupulously careful, however, to avoid the self-help section, which invariably includes manuals on organizing your life, managing your time, setting goals, and other such odious topics.

I really need a closing paragraph for this book. A couple of pithy quotes from some recognized personalities would tie it up nicely, but who? I suppose I could do some research.

Maybe later.